About the Author

Caroline Goyder is a voice, presentation and public speaking expert, and a popular speaker. Caroline has specialised for nearly a decade in helping non-acting clients to perform with poise and power in real life, whether they are delivering a speech, anchoring a TV show, impressing at an interview, or chairing a board meeting. She worked for 10 years as a voice coach at Central School of Speech and Drama, and continues to support clients in business, politics and broadcast with the challenge of communicating with impact in the theatre of life. She is regularly asked to comment in the media on voice and communication issues, and these include *BBC Breakfast News*, *The Speaker*, and *The Voice*. Caroline has also been featured in *The Times*, *The Daily Telegraph*, *The New Statesman*, *The Sunday Times*, *The Guardian* and *The Economist*. Caroline's first book *The Star Qualities* was published by Sidgwick and Jackson in 2009. You can follow her on Twitter @CarolineGoyder and find out more at www.gravitasmethod.com.

For Maggie, Rosemary, Scarlett and Grace

GRAVITAS

Caroline Goyder

How To Communicate
with Confidence,
Influence and
Authority

Vermilion
LONDON

1 3 5 7 9 10 8 6 4 2

Published in 2014 by Vermilion, an imprint of Ebury Publishing
Ebury Publishing is a Random House Group company

The Random House Group Limited Reg. No. 954009
Addresses for companies within the Random House Group can be found at
www.randomhouse.co.uk

A CIP catalog[...] [...] Library

The Random House Group Limited supports The Forest Stewardship Council® (FSC®),
the leading internatio[...] forest-certification organisation. Our books carrying the FSC
label are printed on [...] paper. FSC is the only forest-certification scheme
supported by the lead[...] organisations, including Greenpeace. Our paper
procurement po[...] www.randomhouse.co.uk/environment

Designed and set by seagulls.net

Printed and bound by CPI Group (UK) Ltd, Croydon, CR0 4YY

ISBN 9780091954956

Copies are available at special rates for bulk orders.
Contact the sales development team on 020 7840 8487 for more information.

To buy books by your favourite authors and register for offers, visit
www.randomhouse.co.uk

Contents

Roots and Wings

What Exactly is Gravitas and How Can it Help You Succeed?

Gravity is the ballast of the soul which keeps the mind steady.
THOMAS FULLER, CLERGYMAN AND WRITER

gravitas *n.* figuratively of persons, 'dignity, presence, influence'.

Gravity. Gravitas. The clue is in the name. The Roman virtue gravitas existed long before Isaac Newton named the universal force, but great minds think alike.

Gravitas is about *roots* and *wings*. Roots, because gravitas gives you a solid foundation to express yourself with confidence and authority. Gravitas flourishes when you stop struggling to be someone else and plant deep roots in who you are. Wings, because as G. K. Chesterton put it, 'Angels can fly because they take themselves lightly.'

We can all have gravitas when we speak. The Roman emperor Marcus Aurelius makes it clear: 'Cultivate these, then, for they are wholly within your power: sincerity and dignity … be temperate in manner and speech; carry yourself with authority.' What Marcus understood is that gravitas is a trait – software, rather than hardware.[1] You can learn to carry yourself with authority, to speak with gravitas and confidence, to influence others. You have to know how, of course, and that's what this book is about. It will show you practical steps to take to boost your gravitas today, tomorrow and over a lifetime should you wish.

Gravitas allows you to rise to great heights professionally while keeping your feet firmly on the ground. The world notices your substance as well as your style. We listen to you, remember you and act on your words. When you find your roots and your wings the world sits up and pays attention.

Ancient

Perfect virtue; these five things are gravity,
generosity of soul, sincerity, earnestness and kindness.
CONFUCIUS, PHILOSOPHER

So, what exactly is gravitas?

Gravitas is a Roman word that translates variously as dignity, impressiveness, seriousness, influence, weight and presence. In ancient Rome gravitas was one of the virtues of a good Roman citizen, along with kindness, hard work, self-worth and, crucially, a sense of humour.

Gravitas (or specifically the rhetorical tradition that taught the ancients how to present themselves with gravitas) prior to the arrival of TV and a couple of world wars had been exceedingly à la mode for thousands of years. There was a whole system of voice and body training handed down from Aristotle and Cicero and on via Francis Bacon. It helped people to express themselves with confidence, influence and authority and to succeed in their endeavours.

Gravitas continued to evolve over the centuries and in 1687 it got a rebrand. Isaac Newton published his book *The Mathematical Principles of Natural Philosophy*, in which he explained the universal force and named it gravity, based on the word gravitas. Did this alter our understanding of the original word?

Possibly. It may be that gravitas came to be understood as weightier because of Newton's coinage of the term. And yet it's important to remember that gravity – as Newton explained – is just as up as it is down. Newton's Third Law of Motion describes the nature of opposing forces. For every push down there must be an equal thrust upwards.

Gravitas requires the same balance of forces. The weight of your seriousness must always be balanced equally by your ability to lighten up – humour, humility and wit. Too down and you become all seriousness and there's no spark, no fun, no joy. Too up and you become light as air, insubstantial and no one listens to you because you are not taken seriously.

And then, woefully, for anyone who wanted to learn to express their ideas with clarity and authority, to speak so others listen, the gravitas express hit the buffers in the 20th century, at least as far as the rhetorical tradition that taught the skills was concerned. Helping people speak with power was seen as no longer fit for purpose. The baby of confidence, authority and eloquence was thrown out with the bathwater of elocution. Big mistake.

Modern

A new century brings a new zeitgeist. In the dawning digital age, when talk and talks are ever more important, your gravitas matters more than ever to your success. The 'it' in gravitas, which makes others listen intently, remember you and act on what you say, is a huge asset to success in your work.

A New York think tank recently reported that 67 per cent of senior executives surveyed saw gravitas as the core characteristic of professional presence.[2] Sylvia Ann Hewlett, who commissioned the study, has said that gravitas is 'the elephant in the room, that somehow you have what it takes.' And she adds, 'Our notion of gravitas is changing.'[3]

Hewlett and her team redefined gravitas in the modern world based on survey responses from hundreds of senior executives. The characteristics they placed as being most important for gravitas included being graceful under fire, sticking by your vision, standing your ground and having the emotional intelligence to enable you to bring others round.

None of this would have surprised the ancients. Though Cicero would have phrased it differently and though the challenges of the ancient world have a different hue to those of the modern boardroom or teleconference, the essence of what makes for impact – how you think, how you speak, how you listen, how you move and how you manage emotion – has changed little in thousands of years. That's why the ancient world has some powerful advice for our own age. Because though the world has changed, people haven't. The big difference is that these days the advice is not confined to the elite. It's for everyone with expertise and a reason to share it.

Gravitas is for Everybody

I saw the angel in the stone and carved until I set him free.
MICHELANGELO, SCULPTOR, PAINTER AND ARCHITECT

I want to blow apart the myth that says only the lucky few can have gravitas. Codswallop. *Gravitas is for everybody.* If you have a zone of real expertise and learn to express it with authority, then gravitas is within your grasp.

To find gravitas you sculpt. You chip away at what you don't need (the old anxieties, bad habits of speech and body language, negative beliefs about yourself) until you get to the heart of who you are. And before you start digging deep you need to trust that gravitas is within you. Trust me, it is.

For a long time, most people have believed that gravitas is a fixed quality. I'm here to tell you that it's not. Over a 20-year career working with everyone from schoolchildren and broadcasters to fundraisers and royalty I have seen thousands of people boost their authority and step up in their lives, whether they're landing top jobs, getting elected, winning a pitch, anchoring the news or making a standing ovation-worthy speech.

When it comes to gravitas, it helps to remember the old maxim: 'If you think you can, or think you can't – you're right.' What matters is that you flip the switch on how you see gravitas. When you realise it can be learnt that changes everything.

Carol Dweck, the Lewis and Virginia Eaton Professor of Psychology at Stanford University has shown there are two basic mindsets: there's *static*, where you believe that your intellectual abilities are fixed; and then there's *malleable*, where you believe that your skills can be improved with practice.[4] Studies show that when people believe that a skill is malleable and fluid they score far higher than those who are taught the skill is fixed and unchangeable.[5]

Margaret Thatcher believed and Barack Obama believes that gravitas is malleable. Both were told they lacked authority early on and both did something about it. They obeyed the principles of the growth mindset – *learn, observe, improve*. If you want gravitas make it your mantra.

To help you with that we're going to look at the gravitas equation (see page 9) and the gravitas principles (see Part One, page 21). When you understand them you'll understand that when you know what you're talking about gravitas is well within your reach.

How to Get the Most Out of this Book

Practice isn't the thing you do when you're good.
It's the thing you do that makes you good.
MALCOLM GLADWELL, JOURNALIST AND AUTHOR

There are two ways of using this book. The first is to start at the beginning and work your way through to the end. My hope – and advice – is that you can make time and space for this approach. It's the best way to get a really deep understanding of how the system works so that you can really make it your own.

Though taking the system step by step will allow you to find something that is truly bespoke to you (which makes it very powerful indeed), I know all too well that life can be hectic. If you have a specific need look at the Gravitas Diagnostic section, opposite. It shows you the most important principles to work on based on the challenges you face. And if you need results fast – as we all do when that last-minute presentation or meeting gets sprung on us – then jump straight to Part Two for quick tips and tricks to help you with gravitas in specific situations.

Here's a quick rundown of the book.

First we'll get to grips with the essential *gravitas equation*, which underpins the whole system. It is inspired by the ancient world but I have designed it as a highly practical tool for real life now.

Part One is the path to gravitas. It's a set of seven principles that you can practise in your daily life. You should take some time to read over the principles and to try them out so that you can personalise and own the advice.

You'll find lots of actionable tips and tricks in each principle under *Try This*. The more you do the better you'll get. They are designed to fit into your life – do them little and often.

At the end of each principle you will find suggestions in the *Toolkit* that will help you boost your gravitas in the specific challenges you face. (You will find free videos on www.gravitasmethod.com designed to inspire and supplement your practice.)

After a week of doing a 10-minute daily practice you will notice a difference. After a fortnight your colleagues will notice a difference. After a month the world will notice a difference. My tip: be relaxed and playful when practising because if it's fun you are more likely to continue practising and when you are relaxed you get better results. The weight of gravitas is paradoxical, as we've discovered. You find more gravitas when you relax, enjoy and trust yourself than when you try too hard. So, little and often, with lightness and ease works best in all of the Try This and Toolkit sections.

In *Part Two* we get to the nitty-gritty and look at the *big five* as I call them – the formal *spotlight moments* of life: presentations and talks, meetings, telephone calls and teleconferences, interviews and pitches and being on camera. I tell you what to do, when to do it and the essential top tips to do it well.

Gravitas Diagnostic

The table below will help you work out which chapters will be most useful to you depending on your specific needs.

Over the years I have heard what really worries people about their spotlight moments. These worries are all completely normal. I've listed the tried-and-tested solutions that I've seen work time and time again so you can go straight there if you need to. However, remember that your gravitas will benefit most from going step by step through the book as each one of the seven principles in Part One is an essential part of well-rounded gravitas.

Principle 1: Know Yourself
Principle 2: Teach People How to Treat You
Principle 3: Find Your Voice
Principle 4: Speak So Others Listen
Principle 5: Win Hearts and Minds
Principle 6: Keep an Open Mind and a Level Head
Principle 7: Get Results

Skill You Want	Principles to Focus On
1. Convey passion and energy and secure instant engagement.	1, 5
2. Be authentic in your communication.	1, 3, 6
3. Be convincing in a pitch, presentation or interview.	4, 5, 7
4. Have presence when speaking.	2, 3, 4, 7
5. Make those around you pay attention.	2, 4, 6, 7
6. Project authority.	1, 2, 3, 4
7. Have control and poise when speaking.	2, 3, 4, 6, 7
8. Own opinions and views and make them heard.	1, 3, 6, 7
9. Lean techniques to help you sound and appear more confident.	1, 3, 4, 7
10. Understand and apply the body language of gravitas.	2
11. Handle nerves and stay resourceful in the moment.	6, 7
12. Learn techniques to overcome worries about dealing with people.	6, 7
13. Learn to speak in a deeper voice. Learn how to learn to like your voice.	2, 3
14. Learn how to deal with the moment between being asked a question and responding.	3, 7
15. Engage difficult audiences.	2, 3, 6, 7
16. Communicate with impact on the spot.	3, 4, 7
17. Handle disagreement with aplomb.	6
18. Capture attention and create impact.	1, 2, 3, 4, 5, 7
19. Find calmness when anxiety hits.	1, 4, 6, 7
20. Step up to a big challenge with poise and authority.	1, 2, 3, 4, 7

The Gravitas Equation

How Gravitas Works and How to Find Yours

One cannot lead a life that is truly excellent,
without feeling that one belongs to something greater
and more permanent than oneself.
MIHALY CZIKSENTMIHALY, PSYCHOLOGIST

Before we get into the gravitas principles, you need to understand the gravitas equation that underpins them.

Knowledge + purpose + passion (– anxiety) = Gravitas

This trinity of knowledge, purpose and passion is key. They are the pillars on which gravitas rests. The more you strengthen them the more you find your gravitas. And, unlike many other things in life, these three are enhanced by the passage of time. Let's have a look at how they work.

The Trinity

Knowledge is in your zone of expertise. You must have something to say, a circle of confidence in which you are expert and authoritative.

What most people don't realise (but the ancient world did) is that gravitas is also about knowledge of the *behaviours* of gravitas – the way you express what you know via groundedness, a deep, resonant voice, speaking concisely without fillers, listening fully and having poise under pressure. Body knowledge and mind knowledge need to work together.

Your *purpose* is about your values. Purpose gives you momentum and gravitas shines most when you serve a greater good. This doesn't mean it has to involve UN speeches or leading a nation. All that counts is that it matters to you and to others, so it could be a fundraiser for the school football team or a presidential campaign.

Your *passion* is the spark that sets your ideas and knowledge alight. It fuels you and it inspires and engages others.

The History Bit

The gravitas equation has deep roots, which go all the way back to Aristotle's three pillars of *logos*, *ethos* and *pathos*.[1]

Knowledge or reason Aristotle called logos; character or moral purpose was ethos; and emotion or passion was pathos. These pillars remain essential for impact and gravitas in front of an audience. The ancient Greek version of the gravitas equation would have been:

Knowledge (logos) + purpose (ethos) + passion (pathos) (− anxiety) = Gravitas

There was also a whole system for making sure speakers were vocally and physically calm and in control, aspects of which we will think about later on to help minimise anxiety when it arises.

An Example of a Gravitas Great

Let's look at each of Aristotle's pillars in turn and think about how they show up in one of the 20th-century's gravitas greats – Martin Luther King.

Logos

Logos is about your ideas, your words, your reasoning and how you think and how you express it in writing or in speech. Martin Luther King spoke words that came from deep thinking and reflection and he delivered them in a way that was clear and compelling.

Ethos

Aristotle said ethos – which I've called purpose, and which encompasses your values, your goals and your character – breaks down into three components:

1. Trust and virtue
2. Practical wisdom and credibility
3. Compassion

Trust and virtue are earned over a long time and destroyed in a moment. Wisdom is both intellectual – your circle of expertise, and behavioural – your understanding of how to deliver a message with credibility and power. Compassion is the kindness and empathy that makes for true gravitas and influence as opposed to plain old do-as-I-say authority.

Martin Luther King was a good example of all components of ethos. When you watch footage of his speeches you get a strong sense of his moral values. You trust that what he says is backed up by action. His style is credible and he has compassion. There is warmth in his eyes and his voice tells you that he cares about his audience and his subject matter.

Pathos

Pathos means feeling, emotion. Luther King's speeches had passion and power. Watching footage back you see it in his eyes and you hear it in his voice. He feels deeply about his content and he shares that feeling with his audience to move them to action.

The more you know what to look for, the more you spot the gravitas equation at work in others. When someone is memorable, interesting and subtle you may be in the presence of gravitas. The more you look the more you find it, often in surprising places. You realise that gravitas is a deeply human quality, far more subtle and interesting than in the obvious political arena.

Where your knowledge, purpose and passion meet is your gravitas. If you find that sweet spot then the only interference is anxiety or tension and they're straightforward to deal with if you know how to adjust mind and body.

The Difference that Makes the Difference: The Gravitas Equation in Action

If you're wondering how gravitas can help you in your life, the best way forward is firstly to get to grips with the gravitas equation. Then work out what you're missing and take steps to learn the aspects of gravitas that you most need.

The way forward is different for everyone. It depends on your training and background. If you've trained in a discipline that has made you analytical – say engineering or finance – then you may excel at the knowledge part of the gravitas equation but lack passion.

If you've had more creative training you may be full of passion and purpose but lack the rigour and skill to communicate it powerfully.

If you've just stepped up into a new role you may need to clarify your new purpose – who you are and what motivates you.

The beauty of the gravitas equation is that you can be your own mentor, guiding yourself to the gravitas within.

How the Gravitas Equation Shows Up in Life

Job interviews are a good way to look at how the gravitas equation can help you in life.

Imagine three candidates have reached the shortlist for a job they'd all love to have. In the final round of interviews each candidate has to give a presentation.

Candidate One

He is polished and flashy. He's smooth and he's learnt it, but there's no heart, no soul. All style, no substance. He doesn't get the job.

Diagnosis: He'd benefit from a boost in *purpose*. It would help him find an inner depth to match the smooth surface. He'd inspire people at a deeper level and be more authentic so they'd trust him more.

Candidate Two

She's done lots of homework – it's there for all to see in the script she clutches in a shaking hand and reads verbatim. The content is right but it's dry. There's no connection, no eye contact. It's all thinking with no emotion. She doesn't get the job.

Diagnosis: She'd benefit from a boost in *passion* to engage hearts as well as minds and to be herself, to enjoy the experience more, to minimise the anxiety that blocks her from expressing herself fully.

Candidate Three

She walks in with quiet confidence and stands still and calm. Though a tiny tremor in her voice gives away how much she wants the job it only makes her more human, more interesting because, to borrow from a Leonard Cohen lyric, the cracks are the way the light gets in. Her energy and purpose are what the panel notice. It's as if she reaches out to them and connects, sounding conversational and expert – the pilot of the plane. The audience relax, listen, laugh and trust her. Heart and head, style and substance are balanced. She allows who she is to come through and while her demeanour is warm it also says 'take me seriously'. She gets the job.

Diagnosis: When your *knowledge*, *passion* and *purpose* work together and you rehearse to the point that you can get the nervous butterflies in your stomach flying in formation, that's when you start to take off.

The difference that makes the difference is that gravitas allows you just to be. You don't overdo it with a flashy performance. You don't hide behind a script. You get your thinking clear. You find stillness and calm. You pay more attention to others than to yourself. You focus on serving a purpose bigger than you. And you keep it very, very simple, allowing who you are to come through, trusting that it is enough.

When you find your gravitas and express it in a way that resonates with others your success comes from being who you are.

Field Guide to Gravitas

How to Spot Gravitas in Those Around You – the First Step to Finding it in Yourself

Concision in style, precision in thought, decision in life.
VICTOR HUGO, POET, NOVELIST AND DRAMATIST

I want you to become an ardent gravitas spotter. Have what Albert Einstein called 'holy curiosity' for gravitas when you meet people, watch TV or listen to the radio. It's the essential starting point to finding your own gravitas.

Be warned, gravitas is subtle. And because it won't shout for your attention gravitas takes some discernment to spot.

Coco Chanel believed that failure for a designer is when a couture client walks into a room and everyone says, 'What a dress'. If, however, everyone says, 'Oh you look fabulous' that, for Coco Chanel, was success. Chanel knew that great tailoring enhanced the innate elegance of the person underneath, so that people noticed *them* not the clothes they were wearing.

Ex-White House speech-writer Peggy Noonan says the same is true of good communicators (and people with gravitas): 'You want people to say after hearing you, "She's very intelligent, she made some interesting points."'[1] When gravitas works it reveals you, subtly. Gravitas allows you to know and trust your mind and speak it powerfully so people notice your ideas. Gravitas doesn't shout. It doesn't need to.

Diagnosing this balance in others is the first step. If you can see that broadcaster Y lacks warmth (pathos) or politician X needs a little more clarity of thinking (logos), then you're also more likely to be able to work out what you need yourself.

A Gravitas-spotter's Guide

So that you can start gravitas-spotting, let's have a quick revision of the gravitas equation:

Knowledge + purpose + passion (– anxiety) = Gravitas

If you can see gravitas in others you have the beginnings of finding it in yourself. So let's start looking and we're going to use an exercise to help us do this.

You can do this exercise using a video clip of yourself but it's easiest to observe someone else. (Don't choose an actor in role for this exercise. Gravitas requires people to be themselves. You have to speak your own words.) It's probably easiest if the person is on TV, but they could be in a public space (if you are surreptitious about it) or you could use a radio clip – it's incredible how much you can glean from someone's voice.

When you watch TV or see people present notice how they are doing. Do they have good levels of knowledge, purpose and passion? Is there anything missing? Is their anxiety getting in the way? Start to think about how they would be different with, say, a little more purpose. But remember this is not about perfection. Perfection is deadly dull. The point of gravitas is that it reveals the person, warts and all, and the essential characteristic of gravitas is that the purpose and passion come through and aren't blocked by too much anxiety or self-consciousness. They are who they are. They let it be that simple and that powerful.

Choose someone for this exercise. Watch or listen to the person and ask yourself the series of questions below. You can write your answers down or keep them in your head. If you answer mostly *yes* to these questions then the person has gravitas. If your answers are mostly *no* then they could do with learning the principles in this book.

Knowledge (Logos) Questions

- Are they expert and authoritative?
- Do they have a clear message?
- Does their knowledge extend to their physicality – do they have a body that is grounded and expressive?
- Is their speech clear and well paced – reflecting clear thought?
- Does their thinking seem logical and reasoned, with clear signposts for you to follow?
- Do they use words that fit them rather than just saying what they think they should say?
- Do they take their time, trusting their expertise rather than rushing to get through things?
- Is their pace appropriate to the content? Can you listen fully to each thing they say rather than getting lost because they're going too fast or feeling bored because they're not going fast enough?

Purpose (Ethos) Questions

- Do you get a sense that they are moral and driven by values that serve the common purpose rather than being ego-driven and self-serving?
- Do you trust them? (And whether you do or don't, think about exactly what makes you feel that – their pace, their energy, what they say, how they make you feel?)
- Are they being themselves? Are their inner and outer worlds in tune? (A good guide is how comfortable and relaxed they look in themselves.)

- Do they have credibility and authority?
- Do they have compassion and warmth?

Passion (Pathos) Questions

- Do they care about what they're saying? Are they engaging you when they speak?
- Are they kind, empathetic and attentive to the person/people they are talking to?
- Notice what they make you feel. Is it emotional – excitement or fear? Is it physical – a sense of calm in your body or tension in your muscles? Whatever they feel you feel – pay attention to that.
- Do you breathe deeply when they speak or hold your breath? (This tells you how tense they are as we tend to mirror breathing.) Tension shows you that someone is physically held, rather than released and at ease. They may be masking emotion or feeling anxious or self-conscious.

Managing Anxiety Questions

As we know from the gravitas equation it's not enough just to have knowledge + purpose + passion. **You also have to know how to manage the** *gravitas blockers* **– anxiety and self-consciousness.** This is a skill psychologists call self-regulation.

So something else to look out for on your gravitas field trips is how people deal with stress, anxiety and self-consciousness. If they deal with it well and can stay calm and resourceful under pressure then their gravitas quotient is significantly boosted.

- Are they calm and in control of themselves –aware of the effect they have on others?
- In anxious moments do they bring themselves and others back to calm quickly?

- Are they open and interested in others with minimal ego and self-consciousness?
- Are they able to accept the perspectives of others even when they don't agree with them?
- In a stressful situation, do they have influence – can they work towards a goal and take others with them, adjusting subtly to the views of others?
- Is there a sense that they see themselves as equal to the other person/people (neither looking up nor looking down) and acknowledge the other person/people?
- Do they deal with challenges gracefully? Are they able to adjust their behaviour to the needs of the situation?
- Are they able to push back gracefully and empathetically in moments of conflict?

The more you look for gravitas in the world, the more you see how subtle and powerful it is when it works well. When you start to look for the gravitas equation you start to realise that gravitas is very different to do-as-I-say-or-else cold authority.

What the gravitas equation does is harness all that you are and helps you express it. It connects you to your head and what you think (knowledge), your soul and what you believe (purpose) and your heart and what you feel (passion). When this trinity works together you are authentic and in your element in a way that has real impact in the world around you.

Now let's think about how you can have this gravitas in your own life so that when you speak others listen, and not only do they listen, they act.

PART ONE

The Seven Principles of Gravitas

When I accept myself as I am, I change.

CARL JUNG, PSYCHIATRIST AND PSYCHOLOGIST

Principle 1: Know Yourself

How to Build Your Inner Strength and Stability

We have to stand upright ourselves, not be set up.
MARCUS AURELIUS, ROMAN EMPEROR AND PHILOSOPHER

There is an inscription at the Oracle in Delphi that translates into English as 'Know thyself'. This is the best place to start when it comes to gravitas. Knowing yourself means developing the awareness to recognise thoughts and feelings as they happen. It gives you inner strength and boosts your confidence, decisiveness and grace under pressure.

You'd think knowing yourself would be easy. After all, as the saying goes, 'Wherever you go, there you are.' It's easy to understand the principle but it's much trickier to know yourself in practice, especially in a world that is constantly persuading us that the next big thing is the answer to our dreams and that whispers insidiously in our ear that what we have is not enough. Beware of this voice. It's deeply anti-gravitas. What stops us being self-aware is often anxiety and worry about whether we measure up, whether we fit in. Rather than coming back to what we are, we obsess about what we're not. Constantly chasing after our ideal self makes us dizzily unstable, always seeking the next big thing out there rather than within. The solution is simple. Stop. Pay attention to the possibilities within. Ground yourself in how you are already valuable. Plant roots in who you are. It gives you the stability that is so key to gravitas.

Stable equilibrium is defined in physics as, 'A state in which the body tends to return to its original position after being disturbed.' This inner emotional ballast is fundamental to gravitas. The Sanskrit word 'guru' means 'weighty one', implying someone who cannot easily be knocked over. This stability – emotionally, psychologically, physically – is essential to your gravitas.

I learnt most about this principle from a coach called Yoda (his nickname because of the wisdom he exudes). Yoda transforms the people he works with. From having jerky, twitchy faces and voices and the knee-jerk reactions of people trying to cope with unsustainable workloads and stressful demands, they take on a far more grounded, centred presence. They seem wiser, more resourceful. And they get results. Big time.

So, of course, I asked Yoda his secret. What became clear was that Yoda was teaching his clients that you have to be aware of and able to lead yourself before you can effectively lead others. Think of the calm implacable tones of the leader facing a great challenge or the pilot speaking to the passengers calmly and reassuringly as turbulence hits. Every pilot knows that you have to make sure that you put your own life jacket on before you help others. As the Romans understood very well, your ability to manage yourself is a reflection of your leadership of a wider sphere. If you can be trusted to stand firm under pressure it suggests you might be able to manage others.

Yoda went on to tell me a story about one of the young leaders at managing-director (MD) level. The MD was focused and ambitious and had started to do the mindfulness practice Yoda had suggested for him. At the beginning of each day he'd spend 10 minutes becoming calm and centred.

It paid off. One day he found himself confronted directly by the chairman in a board meeting. Yoda watched as three times the chairman attacked the young MD's ideas. Each time the MD calmly and confidently held his ground, swinging the discussion round to his point of view. The chair, disarmed by the MD's calm, graceful and focused response to his attack, started to listen. He agreed to the MD's recommendations.

Later that day the MD got a call from the CEO of the organisation, who'd watched this exchange of views in the board meeting: 'We've got 10 new jobs going in the management restructure, which one do you want?'

By staying present and steady the MD had communicated his ideas without creating an argument and without caving in. He'd held his ground and found his stability even as the political terrain shifted. He had emanated gravitas. Others noticed and his life changed as a result.

Leadership of the self starts with knowing yourself. As Yoda told me, self-awareness is key:

It helps you find a deep and compassionate centre in yourself where you're not dislodged or anxious because of what's going on around you. You've got an internal source – your capacity, your own intelligence. When you learn to rest into that ... it expresses itself through your voice and your own consciousness.

So, why should something as simple as self-awareness be such a powerful (and professionally promotable) skill? One of the world's leading emotion researchers, Paul Ekman, was puzzled by this question. It was clear that awareness of breath and body was important but he couldn't understand why. Then it struck him. Most of us breathe without thinking, because nature doesn't require us to think about it. What that means is that if we learn 'to focus our attention on breathing ... we develop new neural pathways ... and ... these skills transfer to other automatic processes – benefiting emotional behaviour awareness, and eventually in some people, impulse awareness.'[1]

Ekman's words chime with much of the writing in the ancient world on training of the breath and the body. The ancients saw much of the training they put their athletes and orators through as skills for self-management whether in the arena, in the assembly or in life. When you are aware and in control of your own responses it makes you far better at leadership. Leadership of the self has to come before you lead others.

Science backs up the importance of self-awareness. Research on mindfulness (as this grounded awareness has become known) has shown that it can boost the ability to feel calm, resilient, compassionate and empathetic, as well as improving sustained attention, visual-spatial memory, working memory and concentration.[2] Five days of 20-minute meditations have been shown to reduce anxiety, depression, anger and fatigue and a decrease in the stress hormone cortisol.

Let's look at how you can find ways to bring awareness and steadiness to your own life so you can find your gravitas in challenging situations and achieve success. Physicists will tell you stable equilibrium is all about getting the centre of gravity right. And that's true of gravitas too. So, how do you do it? First you have to have a good level of self-awareness in the mind, an inner spirit level that you steady and a compass to move you forward in the right direction.

Your Inner Compass

Our biological essence, our instinct remnants, are weak and subtle ... the search for spontaneity and naturalness is a matter of closing your eyes, cutting down on the noise, turning off the thoughts, to wait to see what happens, to see what comes.

ABRAHAM MASLOW, PSYCHOLOGIST

The stoic philosophers believed that we all have an inner compass that guides us in the direction of travel that is right for us.

This inner compass is key to gravitas because it gives us stability, resourcefulness and grace under fire. If you're wondering how this compass works look no further than Roman orator Cicero's eulogy for Cato. Cicero tells us that though Cato the Younger, a noted Roman orator was

> born with gravitas, he nurtured it, strengthening it with practice.

Cicero goes on to explain how

> we must decide; *quos*: who we want to be, *quales*: what kind of people, *in quo genere vitale*: in what walks of life ... We should know our particular genius (*ingenium*) and what we are good and bad at and behave accordingly.[3]

Cicero makes clear that if we direct ourselves towards what matters and understand our skills, finding the right home for them in the world, then we are on track with nurturing our gravitas.

We're going to look at how to do exactly that via self-awareness of what you *do*, what you *feel* and what you *think*.

- **Do** How to find a stable base by coming back to the gravity in your gravitas.
- **Feel** How to tune into your gut feelings about what's happening and to let them guide you to your true north – what feels right.
- **Think** Your thinking – what the inner helmsmen of your mind are telling you and how to dialogue with them.

Do: The Gravity in Gravitas

How surely gravity's law ...
Takes hold of even the smallest thing
And pulls it toward the heart of the world ...
This is what things can teach us:
To fall,
Patiently to trust our heaviness.

RAINER MARIA RILKE, *BOOK OF HOURS*

When it comes to the maxim 'Know thyself', that first principle of gravitas, the knowledge must be in the body just as much as in the mind. People with gravitas are present to their physicality as much as to their thinking. It gives them awareness, empathy and speed of response. When you are really *present* to your body, people start talking about *presence*.

Above all you must trust the ground beneath your feet. Anxiety, fear, self-consciousness and tension rise up the body. The simplest and most powerful antidote is to get grounded. That's why gravity, that much maligned field force, is at the heart of gravitas. Gravity gives you gravitas. The stillest person in the room often has the most power and presence.

Be Grateful for Gravity

When the abandonment to gravity comes into action, resistance ceases, fear vanishes, order is regained, nature starts again to function in its natural rhythm and the body is able to blossom fully, allowing the river of life to flow freely through its parts.

VANDA SCARAVELLI, YOGA PRACTITIONER

Gravity is a field force – all around us, unavoidable. The key to accessing the wisdom of the body is to pay attention to the points of support. The field force that is gravity requires contact. A constant supporting force transfers from the earth's surface and supports our weight, from the bones of our feet to bones that are not in contact with the earth. Feeling those points of contact is the focus of the next exercise (see overleaf). It has a powerful effect on your gravitas simply by focusing you on gravity.

Which begs the question – why aren't we all grounded? Modern life has a lot to answer for. We live more in our brains than our bodies. Stress pulls our attention up into the constant whirr of our minds or the incessant buzz of our gadgets. The up direction of anxiety is anti-gravity (and anti-gravitas). Our bodies tense up and hunch over in front of our screens. We carry the weight of the world on our tense, knotted shoulders. We become unstable, our high centres of gravity allowing us to be easily toppled.

And we don't really trust gravity. It hasn't had a very good press. Gravity is seen as such a downer, ageing us with its irresistible pull on our jowls. We're down on down. We forget the support gravity provides – the soothing arms of mother earth, the ground beneath our feet. We're so busy moaning about gravity that we forget how essential it is.

If you want gravitas my advice is to be grateful for gravity. Physics tells us that for every down there must always be an equal and opposing up. Isaac Newton's Third Law of Motion states that 'action and reaction are always equal and always opposite in direction'. Without gravity you wouldn't even be able to stand up. If you weigh 9 stone, when you stand there is a downward thrust of 9 stone. At the same time the floor must push up with a thrust of 9 stone. If it pushed up with 9 stone and 1 pound you'd be airborne.

Try This: Down to Earth – Feet on Floor Bum On Chair

Look well into thyself; there is a source of strength
which will always spring up if thou wilt always look.

MARCUS AURELIUS, ROMAN EMPEROR AND PHILOSOPHER

Laurence Olivier always declined to pass on advice to aspiring actors, except to say, 'Relax your feet.' The following exercise will help you literally to keep your feet on the ground – to find the groundedness essential to gravitas. It is the *do* part of knowing yourself – the ultimate stability in life. You can trust the ground beneath your feet.

The FOFBOC (feet on floor bum on chair) exercise is going down a storm in the schools where it's being taught as an introduction to mindfulness. Whether you're 12 or 52 it is a brilliantly effective practice for moments when you need to come back to a grounded, embodied presence. Try it. You can always have a little Post-it with the mysterious acronym FOFBOC on your computer screen. No one needs to know …

1. As you sit, feeling your FOFBOC, feel your weight. (You can do the exercise standing up, feeling just your FOF.)
2. Notice that you are safe and supported. Be aware of the places you feel pressure – how the body is held and supported by the chair. It's under the bum, the hamstrings and the feet on the floor, the arms on the armrests. Relax and drop where you feel the contact.
3. It can help to visualise that you have tree roots growing down from wherever your body is supported. Imagine that you can draw energy from the ground through your roots. If you can, engage simply with the feelings in your body. Feel the downward weight of

your body, your roots, and then the opposing thrust up, your wings – the opposing forces so key to gravity.

4. Noticing the gentle expansion and contraction of your breathing can be useful.

5. This exercise is something you can do whenever you have a quiet moment. If you can do it for five minutes that's great, but even 30 seconds will help you ground.

(With thanks to Dr Tamara Russell for the FOFBOC exercise.)

Dragon's Tail

If you have a creative mind you may also find the image of a dragon's tail useful. I was taught it at drama school and it really helps you ground. To make it work for you, when you stand or sit imagine you have a long, weighty (scaly if you wish!) dragon's tail that extends out of the base of your spine and curls around you or behind you. It gives you a sense of weight at the base of your pelvis, which helps you feel more stable. If you imagine the tail filling the room it also helps with presence. Strange perhaps, but highly effective – give it a go!

Feel: Find Your True North

If you are to make the right choices for yourself in life – as Cicero suggests Cato did – you need to choose what *feels* right. The US speech coach KC Baker calls this self-direction – steering a course to your true north.[4] True north is best expressed as a this-is-me feeling. Psychotherapist Joseph Campbell had an expression for it: 'Follow your bliss.' Campbell said he came to the idea of bliss via the Sanskrit word *sat-chit-ananda*, which means 'being-consciousness-rapture'.[5]

I don't know whether my consciousness is proper consciousness or not; I don't know whether what I know of my being
is my proper being or not; but I do know where my rapture is.
So let me hang on to my rapture, and let it bring me both my
consciousness and my being.

The good news is that true north – your bliss – is *already there*. It's
always been there. You find it when you express what's already within
you, rather than seeking to impress others. The main practice for
gravitas is to pay gentle attention to true north, moment to moment.
Be aware of what matters to you and what motivates you. What makes
you feel good, in your element. Stay in contact with that bliss and let
it take you step by step to the goals you dream of. Bliss isn't always
blissful of course, it can be hard work. But it's rewarding work, a
feeling of doing what you're here to do.

The thing with true north is that, as Cicero says of Cato, when life
takes you off course you can steer yourself back in the right direction.
You can always shine a light on your integrity and your authenticity
because your instinct leads you there.

Broadcaster and naturalist David Attenborough is a good example
of how true north works for gravitas. Attenborough's gravitas has a
lot to do with his being absolutely tuned in to his innate passion and
purpose, and having headed in the direction of his true north all his
life, building a great body of knowledge en route. David's brother,
director, producer and actor Richard Attenborough said that, 'If you
took a picture of Dave aged 12, it would fit perfectly with what he
is now.'[6] And what boosts Attenborough's gravitas is his clear joy at
sharing his passions. It gives him energy and power as a communi-
cator to be so deeply rooted in his ethos and his values. His values go
through him like a stick of rock.

Finding true north is about tuning into feeling. When you move towards your values you feel good. When you do something that goes against your values you feel bad. Legendary US first lady Eleanor Roosevelt, who chaired the UN Human Rights Commission and helped to draft the Universal Declaration of Human Rights, explains:

> You have to realise what you value most ... comparatively few people ... have paused to consider what had value for them. They spend great effort ... for values that fundamentally meet no needs of their own ... perhaps they have imbibed the values of their particular profession ... their neighbours ... their family. Not to arrive at a clear understanding of one's own values is a tragic waste. You have missed the whole point of what life is for.

The simple, powerful practice of connecting to your values on a daily basis has real power. You can do this by tuning in at the end of each day to what you are grateful for. It teaches you a great deal about your deepest values – very different to those you might have 'imbibed' as Roosevelt puts it.

True north requires that you pay attention to your body and notice whether your choices give you a good feeling – the buzz, the joy of being in your element; or a bad feeling – the low, grey, tired feeling when you're not. Many people choose to live in their heads rather than their bodies, but René Descartes's 'I think therefore I am' is, recent science tells us, not quite right.[7] Feeling matters too. Your emotion and your thinking are inseparably connected. You need to pay attention to both if you are to have the integrity and authenticity of gravitas.

Put Your Brain in Your Belly

They listen to their own voices; they take responsibility …
They find out who they are and what they are … aware, not only
of the godlike possibilities within, but also of the limitations.
ABRAHAM MASLOW, PSYCHOLOGIST

So, how do you tune into your emotions rather than your thoughts? The best advice is what I was taught at drama school – 'Put your brain in your belly'. Strange though the expression may sound, it would have made sense to the ancient Greeks. They said that underneath the diaphragm was a spot called *prapidessin*, which means 'under your crowded thoughts'. This, said the Greeks, was the somatic seat of your intellect – the mental powers and emotions key to understanding. The more neuroscience tells us about the connection between the brain and the gut, the more we realise the Greeks were on to something.[8]

It's a strategy US actor Josh Pais calls 'Ride it don't hide it' – accepting emotion, allowing it to run its course, rather than cutting off from it.[9] His father was a theoretical physicist who worked with Einstein for 11 years. In the summers Josh would go to the laboratory with his dad. Transfixed by the floor-to-ceiling blackboard in his father's lab, covered in calculations, young Josh was perplexed. What on earth was his father doing all day?

At breakfast one day he couldn't contain his curiosity. 'Dad, what do you do? What is your job?'

'Well Joshua, do you see this table?'

'Yes Dad.'

'Do you see your knee?'

'Yes Dad.'

'The smallest part of this table and the smallest part of your knee is made up of the same thing. Atoms.'

'But Dad, what do you *do*?'

'I explore the building blocks of the universe.'

And Josh went off on his bike mulling over the atomic parallels between his knee and the table. Years later as a young actor on Broadway he was struggling with nerves and shyness. Then he remembered his father's words. The body is a mass of atoms just like everything else. He started to see the tense feeling as just a feeling. He removed the labels and levelled down to the sensations he actually felt.

To help us own our feelings rather than hide from them Pais suggests we give the emotion our own nickname. His nickname for insecurity is Mr Mushy. It's much harder to take something called Mr Mushy seriously, which instantly gives you the control back. I was initially pretty sceptical I'll admit, but I've found doing this when I'm hit by negative emotions *really* gives me a bit of distance and some control. When you have good emotions it helps you appreciate and enjoy them. It makes you more self-aware about what makes you tick – the good, the bad and the true north. When you are aware of what is going on, when you know yourself, you make choices informed by your deepest values. Cicero would have approved.

Try This: Tune into True North

Centered is wherever you truthfully are at the time.
JOSH PAIS, ACTOR AND COACH

1. Put your brain in your belly. Identify the feeling you have.
2. Describe the emotion in terms of vibrating atoms, such as swirling, pulsating sickness, churning, heart pumping, jitters.
3. Then 'ride it, don't hide it'. Allow yourself to feel the emotion fully (negative as well as positive). Slow down to take a moment to really feel the sensation.

4. Give the feelings a nickname and let them pass – usually within 7–12 seconds.[10]

If you have to make a decision tune into true north.

- Does this feel right to you? Do you feel positive, light, at ease or a pleasant sense of challenge? Then say yes.
- Do you feel sick, uneasy, a sinking feeling in the pit of your stomach? Then find a way to say no (aka 'ride the no train'). Just make sure you explain why in a way the other person will understand.
- Sometimes of course the decision is out of your hands. If this is the case find a way to make it work for you. Make choices that allow you to find some lightness within it. If it's a presentation you dread doing but there's no way out, then choose the part of it you enjoy or feel good about and start there. Tweak and adjust until you can find the positive within the challenge – the spoonful of sugar that helps the medicine go down. If the decision is about something a few months away make the choice as if you're going to do it today – the helmsman makes a much more accurate decision that way.

Tuning into your values in this way, moment to moment, is absolutely key to gravitas. It fires up the gravitas equation because you stay connected to knowledge, purpose and passion. It ensures that you stay authentic.

Think: The Inner Helmsman

How is my soul's helmsman going about his task?
For in that lies everything.

MARCUS AURELIUS, ROMAN EMPEROR AND PHILOSOPHER

Now, let's think about the *think* part of know yourself. The ancient world understood that we create our world largely by what we think about it and that steering ourselves away from destructive thinking towards productive thinking was key to success and gravitas.

The steering, they said, should be done by your inner helmsman (or helmsmen). I'd like to introduce you to yours so that you can stay on course to true north.

The Voices in Your Head

Your mind will like its habitual thoughts;
for the soul becomes dyed with the colour of its thoughts.
MARCUS AURELIUS, ROMAN EMPEROR AND PHILOSOPHER

Firstly notice that there is a voice in your head. The voice that may well be saying something like, 'A voice in my head, that's not possible'. Thoughts flicker around the mind constantly. Toddlers start by voicing these thoughts aloud; you can hear them talking happily to themselves. Usually we learn later on in childhood to keep these voices to ourselves.

Many of these thoughts, especially when we're anxious or stressed, are self-sabotaging – the graffiti of the brain. Over and over, day in, day out we think the same thoughts. Have you noticed the effect they're having on you? They can be damaging to your gravitas if you don't notice.

For example, as you make a presentation if you are thinking, 'Yes, you fool, you really messed that one up, they are going to find you out' then gravitas has left the building. If, however, you calmly say to yourself, 'Yes, you could have done that better, but stay calm, have a sense of humour about it and you can pull it back' then you're more likely to communicate the poise under pressure so key to gravitas.

Let's think about how you can get a grip on the graffiti.

Critic and Coach

I am not afraid of storms, for I am learning to sail my ship.
AESCHYLUS, DRAMATIST

There are actually a few inner helmsmen in your head when you start to notice them. The two key crew members are your *inner coach* and *inner critic*. You need to be clear with them about their roles.

The coach does *calm* and *celebration*.

The critic does *refinement*. It helps you honestly step up and improve rather than doing full-on character assassination.

When it comes to gravitas the inner critic is useful. Gravitas is not about limitless self-esteem and 'because I'm worth it'. It's grittier and harder-headed than that. The inner critic is an essential tool for gravitas because it allows you to transform, improve and refine. Paulette Randall, theatre director and executive director of the London 2012 Olympic Opening Ceremony explains:

> Gravitas comes with being brave enough to hold a mirror up – to self-examine and question. After a project you have to be able to debrief yourself and look at why things went wrong. Where were you responsible? Not to put yourself down, but to make sure that the next thing you do, you don't make those mistakes again and you put yourself in a better position to do what you've been asked to do. That's hard sometimes because no one can give ourselves as hard a time as we can – nobody – and it's not about giving yourself a hard time – it's just about getting to the point where you can question and ask and then evolve. But it's not always easy.

Try This 1: Meet Your Coach

How do you let yourself know you've done something well? How do you support yourself and give yourself praise? This positive voice is your coach.

- The first step is to notice that you have this voice.
- Say something kind to yourself. Give yourself a bit of praise or positive advice.
- Notice where the voice is, what it says and whose voice it is. Is it yours or a mentor's?
- How does it make you feel?
- Practise turning up the calming voice of the coach whenever you hit anxiety. Notice how it calms you down.

Try This 2: Meet Your Inner Critic

The way to persuade your inner critic out of the dark crevices in which it lurks is to think of a moment where you have felt stressed or under pressure recently. This negative voice you hear in these moments is your critic.

- Notice where the voice is in your head.
- Left or right? High or low?
- Play with the voice, turn the volume down.
- Turn it up so loud it sounds ridiculous.
- Imagine it really far away on a tiny smartphone.
- Notice how when you turn up the inner critic it raises your anxiety levels and stresses you out.

- Notice how when you turn the volume down you relax. In effect, you are in control of how you respond to any situation and if you turn the volume down on the inner critic you can minimise the anxiety that blocks your gravitas.

Use these voices wisely. Sometimes you need to give yourself tough love. But use the critic to make you better not worse. Trust your true north. If all the critic is doing is making you feel bad you need to take it in hand and get it to refine: 'Yes, you could have done that better'; rather than attack: 'You were a disaster'. Know the difference and train your critic to help you.

Try This 3: Get Coach and Critic to Pull Together

Anyone can hold the helm when the sea is calm.
PUBLILIUS SYRUS, LATIN MIME WRITER

Gravitas is a lot about your poise under pressure and when it comes to thinking on your feet the inner critic and coach need to pull together as a crew. The trick to balancing coach and critic is to get them to dialogue. It's the inner version of the angel and devil on each shoulder that you see in cartoons.

- Imagine you have the words 'You don't have any authority/gravitas' echoing round your head.
- Interrogate it. Turn the 'You don't' into an 'If'. You ask your brain to consider the alternatives. Question: 'If you did have authority/gravitas what would you do differently?' Or 'If you knew you had authority, what would you be doing differently?' You can play with the question.

- Depending on the questions you've asked yourself, your answers may be something like, 'I would be more relaxed and speak with more power' to the strategic/practical, 'I'd sign up with a coach' or 'I'd speak with more confidence'.
- You can also talk back to your critic. If your critic says, 'You're going to mess this presentation up' talk back to it with the kind voice of the coach. You might say, 'What if it goes well? You did it well last time.'

The more you get the critic and coach to talk to each other, the more they pull together.

Principle 1: Know Yourself Toolkit

One must be willing to have a knowledge of oneself …
You must try to understand truthfully what makes you do
things or feel things. Until you have been able to face the
truth about yourself you cannot be really sympathetic or
understanding to what happens to other people.
ELEANOR ROOSEVELT, FIRST LADY OF USA

Do: Remember FOFBOC

Physical grounding allows you to tap into your deepest intuition. Feet on floor, bum on chair (see page 30) – make it a regular practice. Feel your body making contact where it is supported. Drop into the force of gravity and feel how the downwards force also has an up.

Feel: True North

In addition to the exercises already mentioned in this chapter, another way to tune into what makes you glow with life, to recognise your deepest values, is to play the What's your Sentence? game. Clare Boothe Luce, one of the first women in US Congress, said to John F. Kennedy that a great person 'is one sentence'. Franklin Delano Roosevelt's sentence was that 'He lifted us [the US] out of Depression and won a war'. Abraham Lincoln's was 'He preserved the union and freed the slaves'. What's your one-liner? Or rather, what would you like it to be? It can give you an inkling as to your true north if you're curious about it.

Think: Balance Your Inner Critic and Coach

Know when to refine and when to celebrate. Find the balance – it will give you honesty, humility and instinct.

Let Self-Knowledge Develop Slowly

It's a lifetime's work – an emergent wisdom that just goes on getting better with time. Eleanor Roosevelt explained it well:[11]

> This self-knowledge develops slowly … but if you keep trying honestly and courageously, even when the knowledge makes you wince … even when you rebel against it … it is apt to come in flashes of insight. 'Oh so that is why I did that' … or 'Now I see why I was afraid to do that!'

Dual Attention

As you explore new aspects of yourself, the unexplored parts of you, be wary of what Eleanor Roosevelt calls becoming 'completely absorbed in your self-study'. Keep it 50/50. Give 50 per cent of your attention to your inner helmsman, in mind and body, and 50 per cent to the world, learning and listening. This dual attention keeps you aware and open to what happens around you. It boosts your presence, your empathy and your influence. And, of course, your gravitas.

Principle 2: Teach People How to Treat You

How to Balance Status and Connection So Others Respect You and Like You

No one can make you feel inferior without your consent.
ELEANOR ROOSEVELT, FIRST LADY OF USA

The ancient world understood very well that we teach others how to treat us. Decorum was the Roman word for getting the right style for the occasion. In modern life decorum matters too. If you walk into a room with calm authority and confidence you will be treated with respect. If you scuttle in nervously you shouldn't be too surprised if you get a less positive response. It's up to you.

You need to be like the pilot of the plane. We need to know we are safe in your hands. A client of mine found himself on the gallery at Gatwick Airport in the UK 20 years ago, listening to pilots communicating with the air traffic control tower. Two decades later he can still recall the calm, low, resonant voice of a Chicago-bound American Airlines' pilot. The feeling of safety and security that voice communicated is something that he remembers to this day. A voice that said 'You are safe in my hands'.

What made the pilot so memorable was his ability to communicate, via the voice alone, the balance between his credibility – his status as an expert pilot – and the care for and connection he had with his passengers. That balance is what I want to explore with you in this chapter. What does your style tell others about you? Are you the pilot of the plane in life, credible and authoritative? Or are you the air steward, friendly and accommodating?[1]

In particular, what you need to understand is that you can change gear between *status* (pilot of the plane) and *connection* (friendly air steward). These are straightforward gears that we can all access. They are practical and will help you step up your gravitas and your power instantly in a way that is friendly and you.

In this chapter we'll think about whether you are habitually more pilot or more air steward and we'll diagnose how best to boost your gravitas and to find the holy professional grail of *credible passion*. Sometimes adjustments need to happen in the space of a morning – going from an informal team briefing to a board meeting requires a shift in style. Once you have these gears you can switch them on and off at will.

Then you can be credible – the pilot of the plane – when others require it of you, and shift gear into approachable air steward when the responsibility is on someone else's shoulders. Let's have a look at how it works.

The Power of Credible Passion

I have a belief – we teach people how to treat us.
INDIGO WILLIAMS, PERFORMANCE POET

Gravitas isn't a constant. It's fluid, ebbing and flowing. As sociologist Max Weber said about charisma, your gravitas is endowed on you by your audience, moment to moment. When you understand the dynamics of decorum you can subtly change gear to keep your audience's attention.[2]

When it comes to getting the balance right between credibility and approachability you can learn a lot from good newsreaders. They have to get the balance between 'take me seriously' and 'warm, compassionate human being' just right. Every night. They have a term for it – credible passion. Credible passion (or credible *com*passion if you prefer) is the gravitas equation in action – your knowledge and your passion combined.

The Status Connection Scale

So, how do you find your credible passion?

Well, you need to know how status and connection work together then you can use them to find the right style to suit the moment. Deborah Tannen, professor of linguistics at Georgetown University in the USA, has done much of the research on status/connection.[3] Her theory is that status and connection are two ends of a scale.

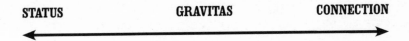

STATUS   **GRAVITAS**   **CONNECTION**

Each end of the scale has its own behaviours. The table overleaf gives a quick summary of what you can expect to find at the extreme end of each. Of course, we all do a combination of these behaviours. The aim of the table is to help you to map the differences so you can see the styles at play in others and to diagnose the required decorum for situations that you face.

	Status (King/Queen and Warrior)	Connection (Carer and Creator)
Values	Respect	Friendship
Decision style	Makes own mind up	Asks advice
Style	Authority	Empathy
Focus	Task	Relationship
Speaking style	Report-talk (sounds authoritative)	Rapport-talk (sounds approachable)
In a team	Competitive	Collaborative

Status or Connection?

So, what's your style?

We can all do both but sometimes we get stuck in one style. To unstick yourself you need to know your current habit. The following questionnaire will help you to do this.

It might be that working in a formal environment has taught you to do too much status. Or maybe you've been in a caring role and you've become very connection in style. To decide whether you are currently more of a status player or a connection person do this quick question-naire using the following question as its basis:

Which statement is most like you at work?

	Column A		Column B
1.	Want to be credible, respected	or	Want to be likeable and empathetic
2.	Focus on precision and getting the job done	or	Focus on the people and the relationship
3.	Analytical and objective	or	Instinctive and emotional
4.	Formal in style – body is upright and owns space	or	Informal and chatty in style – body is fluid, allow others to take up space
5.	Direct: tell people what needs to be said in a straightforward way	or	Indirect: speak empathetically, tuning in and adapting to what people want to hear
6.	Tend to influence more by push than pull	or	Tend to influence more by pull than push
7.	Voice tends to be lower	or	Voice tends to be warmer and melodic
8.	Focus on the big picture, the goal – steps back	or	Focus on the people
9.	Comfortable in formal situations where you can play your power	or	Comfortable in informal situations where you can build relationships
10.	Still and don't do much social smiling – comfortable with pauses	or	Warm and mobile, lots of nodding and smiling to make others comfortable – fill a pause

Count up how many of your answers are from column A and how many from column B.

Mostly A answers: Your habit is to be more *status* in life and you need to find the *connection* side of you to truly find your gravitas.

Action step: Go to How to Do More Connection (Carer and Creator) (see page 55) and look at the tips. Try them in safe places and then apply some of them when you need more compassion and empathy – when relationships matters more than getting the job done.

Mostly B answers: You tend to do more *connection* in life and you will benefit from learning how to play more *status* to boost your gravitas.

Action step: Go to the How to Do More Status (King/Queen and Warrior) (see page 52) and look at the tips. Try them in safe spaces and then incorporate some of them when you need more credibility.

Mix of A and B answers: Your *status* and *connection* are in balance – a great foundation for gravitas.

Action Step: Hone both How to Do More Status (King/Queen and Warrior) (see page 52) and How to Do More Connection (Carer and Creator) (see page 55) with a focus on situations that you find particularly challenging. Pay attention to what happens to you when you are anxious or highly stressed. Do you have a default position?

Flex Your Style

Status and connection are traits. You can change them if you wish. The art when it comes to style is to be able to *flex*. As Deborah Tannen says, there's no right or wrong:

> Although I personally prefer my own style, which makes the most sense to mé – I do truly believe that all styles are equally valid as styles, and that they can work well in some situations ... But that does not mean that all styles work well in every situation. In the end the best style is one that is flexible.

If you're a senior politician, your version of credible passion will be higher on authority with a dash of warmth to signal that there is a nice human being underneath the seriousness of the job. Whereas if you're a primary school teacher, you might front up the likeability but show the inner steel of your authority whenever you need to assert some boundaries behaviour-wise in class. It's about balancing the subtle requirements of the job, and the person that you are, and finding the mix of authority and likeability that works at any given moment.

Archetypes: Four Gears for Credible Passion

Archetypes are a brilliant way to test out your flexing muscles because the thing with archetypes is that they are already there, waiting for you. The word archetype comes from the Greek word meaning imprint or mould. An archetype is something that is innate within you. When you say to children, 'Act like a queen' they sit up and look regal.

Overleaf, to help you flex your status and connection style, is a table detailing four key archetypes: king/queen, warrior, carer and creator. Gravitas requires a healthy balance of all four. When you look for these in the world you will find that people with gravitas are often very strong in all four and are able to use them flexibly.

The top half of the table is the *ruler* (authority) archetypes and the bottom half is the *carer* (likeability) archetypes. The top half is all authority, the bottom half caring creativity.

On the left-hand side are the *static* archetypes – they are cool and objective in mood and style (think yin energy); on the right are the *dynamic* archetypes – they are active, driving, motivating in style (think yang energy).

The top row is the *status* archetypes. The bottom row is the *connection* archetypes.

	STATIC	DYNAMIC
STATUS	**King/Queen**	**Warrior**
	Examples: Barack Obama, Queen Elizabeth II. **Style:** Wise, reasoned, objective. **Where to use it:** When you need to step back, see the bigger picture, be an objective, respected leader. **Actions:** • Step back; be objective, analytical. • Voice is calm, reflective. • Voice in the head. • Stay cool and calm no matter what. • Poker face. • Formal body language and dress.	**Examples:** Malcolm X, Margaret Thatcher. **Style:** Drives change, action focused, challenging. **Where to use it:** When you need to move things forward, make bold changes, lead from the front. **Actions:** • Focused on action and task. • Staccato, punchy gesture on key words. • Voice in the gut. • Grounded and in the body.
CONNECTION	**Carer**	**Creator**
	Examples: Oprah Winfrey, Nelson Mandela. **Style:** Supportive, empathetic, builds a team. **Where to use it:** Where people need to be heard and supported. Where you need to pull together. **Actions:** • Speak from the heart – warm voice, honest, authentic speech. • Eyes are soft, smiling. • Empathetic. • Voice in chest, melodious, full of emotion. • Allow yourself to be vulnerable where you can; disclosure.	**Examples:** Billy Connolly, Dustin Hoffman. **Style:** Humour, originality, inspiration. **Where to use it:** To energise, enliven, inspire, to make people laugh. **Actions:** • Eyes are shining, full of energy and enthusiasm. • Big picture, vision, inspire. • Sparky, quirky, dynamic. • New ideas, loves change. • Voice and gesture highly expressive. • The visual matters – stylish and idiosyncratic.

Try This: The Status-Connection Experiment

The art to these archetypes is first to notice how they show up in you and in others. Notice your habits. Watch yourself on video if you're not sure. If you work in a very formal environment you may have got into the habit of playing king/queen. If you are in an informal, creative, entrepreneurial environment you may have developed a strong warrior-creator. A parent returning to the workplace after time looking after young children may be a very strong carer.

However, you will be pleasantly surprised at how straightforward the status and connection gears are and before we go any further I want you to discover just how quickly you can change gear.

In this exercise you're going to record yourself saying the days of the week first with your palms up and then with your palms down.

1. Take your phone and find the voice recording function (or the video camera is fine too – you can just record your voice).
2. Press record.
3. Say the days of the week as you gesture at stomach height with your palms up.
4. Say the days of the week as you gesture at stomach height with your palms down.
5. Play it back.
6. Notice the difference in voice tone. The palms-up voice will sound higher, more musical – more *connection*. You will sound more *carer* or *creator*, depending on how static or dynamic you are.
7. The palms-down voice is lower, more *status*. It will be more *king/queen* if you are calm, more *warrior* if you are in a punchy mood.

Why the Difference?

It's interesting how the palms help you change gear so quickly from status to connection isn't it? It's all in the wrists.

- **Status** The palms-down gesture is the physiology of control and task. It's why politicians try to get their hand at the top of a handshake, palm down and why they pat each other on the back. Palm down says power. The voice has low authoritative tones that tell you what to do and help you to take the person seriously.
- **Connection** The palms-up gesture is the physiology of surrender, openness and trust. The wrists are a very vulnerable part of the body and revealing them signals openness. That's why when you use the palms-up gesture the voice usually has more warmth and connection. It sounds more approachable.

How to Do More Status (King/Queen and Warrior)

The status end of the continuum is pure credibility and the word credibility comes from the Latin *credere*, meaning to believe, to trust. Sometimes status is essential. In teaching they say, 'Don't smile before Christmas'. It's a joke, of course, but like all jokes there's a deep truth within it. Until people trust you there's no point trying to be their friend.

Sometimes an audience is looking to you to be the pilot of the plane, to take charge. In those moments the worst thing you can do is try to be friendly with them. Major-General Jonathan Shaw was the head of Counter Terrorism at the MoD and he makes a good point about leadership: 'An audience is not just listening to the words, they're also listening to the tone, they're making a human judgement. Is this person talking with any authority, do I need to listen to them?'

Try This: Status Tips and Tricks

The trick with playing status is to keep your natural warmth running through. Make status about working towards a common good. Status is like chilli pepper, sometimes you don't need very much to get the effect you want. Learn to play it in subtle doses.

Do the Power Pose

The first step to status is to stand and sit well. Posture matters to playing status. Dana Carney and her colleagues from Columbia and Harvard universities wanted to explore if certain body language increased feelings of power. Their thesis was that since humans and other animals express power through open body language and express powerlessness through closed postures, might it be that taking up open postures actually cause power?

It worked when the researchers asked volunteers to take up a power pose (standing tall, taking up space), the volunteers felt more 'in charge' and 'powerful' and showed significant increases in testosterone to match their 'I feel in charge' feelings. Plus the high-power poses also made the people who held them feel better. They measured lower on adrenalin and cortisol – the stress hormones. Carney concluded, 'That a person can, by assuming two simple 1-min poses, embody power and instantly become more powerful has real-world, actionable implications.'[4]

So, make it work for you. When you need a confidence boost, stand tall. Pull yourself up to your full height. Get some backbone. It's all there in our language – sometimes you have to find the outer physicality first, and let the thinking follow.

Focus on Task, Not Relationship

If you want to play status get straight to the point, straight to the task. Status players respect someone who focuses on getting the job done rather than on trying too hard to be their friend. Avoid social smiling. Where you need more credibility only smile if it happens naturally. And avoid doing too much raised 'like me' eyebrows. Relax your eyebrows.

Minimise Nodding

Where authority and credibility matter, replace nods with stillness. To play power, keep your head still and relaxed, as long as you can do it with ease. It should be a graceful, attentive stillness (it should not look like you're wearing a neck brace).

Cut Fillers

'Ums', 'ers', 'I think' and all those other clunky fillers we use lower our status because they give away the fact that we're not comfortable with a pause. Get comfortable with a pause. Don't fill it, just chill, and if in doubt relax your face and remember to breathe.

Do Newsreader Resolved Intonation

For status, channel the newsreader's voice. At the end of the line drop the pitch. 'Here is the [drop the note] news.' (The opposite – connection central – is when the note goes up at the end of the line and it sounds like a question.)

Don't Go Overboard

Even the military – the profession that above all others you'd think would advocate a tell 'em what to do style – doesn't think that all push, all credibility, makes for lasting influence. In our interview Major-General Jonathan Shaw made the interesting point that actors often get soldiers wrong, 'They put on this mantle of over-assertiveness, "I'm the boss"… It's not like that. They try too hard. Too much effort.'

___

So, feel free to play with these status tips and tricks but treat them like a strong spice – use them with care. If you are with uber-status players – the chairman of the board, say – then go all out on task. Otherwise keep the elegant balance of credible passion. Let's add the connection style to help you do just that.

How to Do More Connection (Carer and Creator)

There is no influence, no true gravitas without connection. You just have to get it balanced right with status. I love the Greek word for connection, *eunoia*, which translates as beautiful thinking or goodwill. It's so important to have that glow of warmth that gives your listeners the strong sense that you have their best interests firmly at heart. Without that warmth, authority can quickly become authoritarian.

___

Try This: Connection Tips and Tricks

Presence is not just versatile; it's also reactive. Certain people, we say, 'command attention' but the verb's all wrong. There is no commanding, only soliciting.
MALCOLM GLADWELL, JOURNALIST AND AUTHOR

Focus on Relationship, Not Task

Anxiety can make status players very task focused and it shows up in your eyes. People can see you're not listening and they can feel hurt by it. Let go of the job you have to get done for a moment and make time for the person you're with.

Be Informal

Be informal in the way you hold yourself. Put your weight on one foot or the other, and lean forward. Think fluid, expressive mode.

Lighten Your Expression

Monitor your screen-saver face (in photos, in the mirror, in shop windows). If you tend to look a little serious start to greet people with a real smile in your eyes.

See People as Old Friends

Imagine people you meet are old friends. Be pleased to see them. Make sure that you have a listening face that is warm and interested (check this in the mirror some time if you're not sure).

Be Fascinated

Everyone is fascinating. Find out what you can. Ask questions about their lives. Listen to and remember their answers.

Your Stretch Zone

Think about where your stretch zone is. By this I mean think about which archetypes make you feel less than comfortable. Where do you feel out of place? Perhaps there is one archetype that you only use when talking to friends or family. What if you brought more of, say, the carer, or the creator to work? What would be different? Try them out in safe places. Children's bedtime stories are the perfect place to test them if you are a parent.

Once you know what your tendencies are you need to think about what will make your audience feel at home. A very formal audience will value you starting out as a king or queen. You'll need to make sure you obey the protocol and are dressed to the manner born. If you are talking to a group of students, you might relax your style and be more of the carer/creator. If this part of you doesn't normally show up in professional situations you are likely to need to practise it a little in the mirror at home, or film yourself, or even get a friend to give you feedback.

Essentially, use a blend of these archetypes most of the time. It's a good way to keep your gravitas dynamic and engaging. If you realise that the audience's eyes are no longer shining that is your signal to change gear fast. When you notice attention has dimmed, it's up to you to get it back.

Preview Your Style

Imagination is everything.
It is the preview of life's coming attractions.
ALBERT EINSTEIN, THEORETICAL PHYSICIST

If you want to step up your style and boost either your authority or your likeability it can help to take the same approach as you do with sartorial style. First, visualise how it might look, then try it on to see if it fits and if it suits you. Only then do you present it to the world.

The art to finding the right style for the right moment is your ability to read the situation and then to choose the perfect blend of authority and likeability. It's the same instinct that helps you get a dress code right. Too conversational a style in a formal situation makes the audience worry that you aren't prepared or aren't respectful of your surroundings. Too formal in a relaxed environment and you seem stuffy and inflexible. Subtle adjustments are required for each situation.

First diagnose the need then prescribe the precise balance required. If you don't know the individuals involved, do your research. Look at the website. See if you can find them on YouTube. Talk to them. Find out the style that they use and then work out the style you need to communicate to them. It's not about being a carbon copy, more about finding your version of their style. We like people like us, or people we want to be like.

As a rule of thumb, if it's formal you might go for 70 per cent king/queen – still, upright, low vocal tone, with 30 per cent carer – a smile on your face and a warmth in the eyes. If it's an informal setting with people you know well you can turn up the dial on carer/creator, say to 60 per cent, so you are chatty and fluid, with palms up and the voice musical, with just enough king/queen to help your audience trust that you're in charge. Of course what really matters is how you respond in the moment. As the army say, 'No plan survives contact with the real world'. You will adjust to circumstance, but at least you will be prepared.

Try This: Style Preview Exercises

1. **Make the movie** Visualisation is your secret weapon. It's the best way to quickly and effectively focus on the style of delivery you want. Researchers at Carnegie Mellon and the University of Pittsburgh in the USA have shown that how well you mentally rehearse a task affects how well you perform it. Rehearsal allows you to activate the brain's essential prefrontal cortex in advance. If you can imagine it, it's easier to do for real.[5]

2. **Hear it back** Use your phone/camera to try king/queen and carer separately. Listen back and test out combinations of credibility and compassion. The palm-up or -down gestures will help – strange but true – you'll hear them change your voice.

3. **Check in the mirror** Test the archetypes in a mirror. You'll probably notice that there's a difference between what it feels like and what you can see happening. Reset your inner gauge and keep reminding

yourself that what you feel inside is sometimes not what others see on the outside. If in doubt, check.

4. **Take it into the world** Try it where not a soul knows you so they don't have grounds for comparison – in the supermarket, at the airport or when you ring a call centre.

5. **Test it for real** Once you've been through these stages try it out at work. First with people who don't know you well, in low-stakes situations. If it works, you can start to feed it into the high-stakes moments.

Master the Art of Informal

When you get these style gear shifts in the muscle you will start to be able to play, to break the rules a little. This is when gravitas really flies. Ours is a tricky age, seeming informal, but requiring subtle formality. 'Fireside chats' are the norm. Philosopher, writer and broadcaster Alain de Botton gave me his advice for negotiating the smart-casual of communication.

The good speaker needs to negotiate the issue of authority. An aristocratic age accepted hierarchy: he is talking, they have to listen. Nowadays, you have to lure your audience into forgetting that you have the pulpit, that you have power over them. You have to sound like an ordinary fellow egalitarian citizen, who has simply managed to capture their attention. [This] quietly concealed authority is achieved by someone suggesting that they are essentially just like the audience, an ordinary person, they just happen to be on stage. This is an artful lie, sustained by such techniques as speaking in an apparently casual way, stumbling a little – in a highly controlled manner – seeming to lose the plot every now and then, but not doing so. In other words, faking being an amateur while being a total professional: that is the peculiar demand of our democratic age.

Principle 2: Teach People How to Treat You Toolkit

*Life is like riding a bicycle – you have
to keep moving to find your balance.*
ALBERT EINSTEIN, THEORETICAL PHYSICIST

The best style is the style you don't notice.
SOMERSET MAUGHAM, NOVELIST AND PLAYWRIGHT

Balance Status and Connection

Report-talk or rapport talk? Credibility or approachability? King or queen/warrior or carer/creator? Know your audience and find the style that communicates best. For status and credibility, focus on the task and be objective, analytical. For connection, focus on relationship and connect emotionally and empathetically.

Separate Style from Identity

Remember that just as you can dress formally or informally and still be yourself, you can choose whether to be the pilot of the plane or the air steward and still be yourself. It's as much about making others feel comfortable as anything else.

Visualisation

Use visualisation as a tool to help you prepare your style for an audience. Taking five minutes the day before to visualise how you want to be – credible with a smile, say, or warm and friendly, or highly focused and formal – can help you actually do it for real.

Keep it Simple

Coco Chanel used to say that the secret of style was to remove one accessory or item of clothing before leaving the house. This principle works well for communication too. Choose one thing to focus on each day – stillness, an awareness of building relationships, really listening, playing your power posture. Notice how it works for you and let it drop into the muscle, another part of the unconscious toolkit. Ease and elegance are what it's about.

Principle 3: Find Your Voice

How to Communicate with Originality and Clarity

Finding a voice means that you can get your feeling into your own words, and that your words have the feel of you about them.
SEAMUS HEANEY, POET

If you've ever struggled to get thoughts from your brain out eloquently into the world while listening enviously to others who effortlessly rise to the challenge, take heart. The way you communicate in speech and in writing is something you can improve far more easily than you realise.

Eloquence means, simply, 'the communication to an audience of all a speaker has in their mind'. This direct line from your mind to the ears or eyes of your audience is a key to the honesty and authenticity of gravitas. When you speak or write from the heart, clearly and powerfully, that's compelling. It makes others want to pay attention because they sense that the inner and the outer are communicating directly. What we see is what we get. We trust you.

Eloquence is something that improves with practice, whether you want eloquence in writing or in speaking. The focus of this book is on speaking, but good writing helps you order your thoughts, and ordered thoughts make for good speech.

So, how do you do it? First, you need to *find your original voice* as a speaker (and writer) and to express it with sincerity. You need to be very clear about your zone of expertise and humble about what you don't know.

Second, you need to know *how to communicate these thoughts* in a way that is measured and clear. This is the art of distillation, the art of the precis, of cooking your ideas down to a perfectly digestible form for your audience.

Third, you need to *internalise it, get the ideas by heart* so that you can be natural. Yves Saint Laurent said that elegance is forgetting what you're wearing. Speaking well requires a similar ease. And ease, to paraphrase the Augustan poet Alexander Pope, comes from art not chance, 'as those who move easiest were taught to dance'.[1]

Sound Like You: The Art of Sifting

Your true sound ... takes time to locate ... it's delicate.
You're pursuing self-awareness while fighting off self-consciousness
... You don't want to sound like other people, you want
to sound like you, only a better, clearer you.
PEGGY NOONAN, EX-WHITE HOUSE SPEECH-WRITER

Voice, says the *Oxford Dictionary*, is 'a particular attitude, opinion or feeling that is expressed; a feeling or opinion that you become aware of inside yourself'. People with gravitas express that opinion clearly, gracefully and empathetically. You have to be aware of your thoughts and then voice them in an ordered way.

Eleanor Roosevelt used to say that one of her most important lessons at school came when an English teacher tore up one of her classmate's exam papers saying:[2]

You are giving me back what I gave you ... and it does not interest me. You have not sifted it through your own intelligence. Why was your mind given to you but to think things out for yourself?

Eleanor Roosevelt concludes:

> What counts in the long run is not what you read; it is what you sift through your own mind ... it is the ideas which are a reflection of your own thinking which make you an interesting person.

This lesson is absolutely central to gravitas. Speech, as Seneca put it, is the 'mirror of the mind'. The more you tend to your original thinking, the better chance you have of communicating something worth listening to. Sifting is the ability to filter your ideas through your own mind before expressing them to others. Few people sift. Most people regurgitate ideas they've read, seen or heard others regurgitate. It's hard when we have so many attitudes swirling around our culture. We absorb them without noticing, even though we may not, at heart, agree with them.

Try This: How to Sift for Originality

If people are thinking for themselves about the things that matter to them, I am fascinated. You can tell when a person has moved from let-me-please-you thinking back to their own mind. They go from soporific to scintillating just like that.
NANCY KLINE, AUTHOR, TEACHER, COACH AND PUBLIC SPEAKER

Read
Monitor the quality of what you read. Reading the original thoughts of others, when they're of good quality, inspires your own thinking.

Output takes input. Peggy Noonan lays down the law:[3]

> Reading is the collection of intellectual income, writing the spending of it. You need to read to write, you need to take in

other people's words, thoughts and images. If you want to be a good conversationalist, you must both talk and listen.

It's evident as soon as someone opens their mouth how widely they read and how much they think. Feed your brain and your gravitas will grow. It's simple – you need to read widely and absorb new words and ideas like a sponge.

Write

A very good way to find words that have the feeling of you is to make morning pages a regular practice. Morning pages is a classic practice for writers to find their voice. It comes from the work of Julia Cameron, the author of *The Artist's Way* (Pan, 1995 – a great book, well worth investing in). By writing something original totally instinctively and fluidly each day you start to tap into your true voice. Then you find it happily shows up for you in other parts of your life.

I started doing morning pages when I was in a job I hated. A wise friend whose mother is a writing teacher suggested morning pages as a good way to get my stress out on the page. A year after doing the morning pages I was on my way to becoming a published author. Try it. I hope it has a similarly powerful effect on you.

On waking (or if mornings are not realistic find 10 minutes at the end of the day or even on a commute if you can find somewhere to sit down quietly) write for 10 minutes. Don't analyse, just write, allow the words to pour out of you, a complete stream of consciousness. You don't even have to read it again, but it connects you to a channel of energy that you can come back to.

What you will find is that when you do this regularly your voice as a writer or speaker will emerge as you tap into the unconscious mind where your voice resides.

Splurge it all out and never look at it again. Lock it in a cupboard, burn it if you must. It's about the writing not the reading. It's about the process and what it releases – your voice, not the product.

Speak

Who dares not speak his thoughts is a slave.

EURIPIDES, DRAMATIST

You can also sift as a speaker. Abraham Maslow (the father of humanistic psychology) was once at a party when he had a big insight regarding let-me-please-you thinking.[4] Pouring himself a drink Maslow found himself congratulating his hostess on choosing a very good Scotch.

He then had an epiphany:

What was I saying? I knew very little about Scotches. All I knew was what the advertisements said. I had no idea whether this one was good or not; yet this is the kind of thing we all do.

You've probably done the same, I know I have. Speaking to fill silence, saying things you don't really mean – audible filler. It's not a cardinal sin, but it's not very gravitas and it's not authentic. It's good to learn how to stop it when you want to switch on authority and be true to what you *really* feel.

Maslow gives you some steps to help, using wine as a metaphor, but it can work for *anything* you have an opinion about whether it's Wagner or wellies.

1. Do not look at the label on the bottle (it shouldn't be a cue about whether or not you should like it).
2. Close your eyes. 'Make a hush'. Shut out the world.
3. Savour the wine on your tongue.
4. Look to the 'supreme court' inside yourself.

5. Then, and only then may you come out and say, I like it, or I don't like it. And say what *you* think.

Try it. You'll be amazed at what you discover about yourself when you avoid regurgitation. After a while it feels much better to voice what you really think. The interesting thing is that others sense this and respond much more positively. The things that we think are quirky or weird are often the really human, honest parts that others relate to.

When a speaker is honest, imperfect and funny we relax a little in our shared imperfections, we stop trying to pretend. When you find your true voice we gravitate to you and we endow you with gravitas.

I Believe

Above all, when it comes to sifting keep asking yourself, 'What do I believe?' KC Baker (see www.kcbaker.com) suggests writing down five beliefs (i.e. 'I believe that gravitas is something that everyone can learn. We can all carry ourselves with authority.' Or 'I believe that no one can make you feel inferior without your consent.') These beliefs give a backbone to your original voice and they often become a great template for talks, presentations and blogs. Connect them to your stories, particularly around your eureka moments or epiphanies when you learnt them. This gives you great, authentic content – a huge boost to your gravitas.[5]

Know Your Limits

True experts recognise the limits of what they know and what they do not know. If they find themselves outside the circle of competence, they keep quiet or simply say, 'I do not know'. This they utter unapologetically.

ROLF DOBELLI, *THE ART OF THINKING CLEARLY*

Bluffing and blagging does not make for gravitas. The rule of gravitas is: *know what you know, know what you don't and know the difference*. As Simon Jack, business and economic presenter on the BBC Radio 4 *Today* show told me when we spoke about his interviews with senior business leaders:

> Authoritative people are … thoughtful – they don't just hare off on subjects they don't know much about. If they do come across something they don't know about, they're the ones who will say.

How you respond to difficult questions is a great test, it's where you see the difference between someone who can act expertly and someone with real depth. When your expertise is so in the muscle that it goes through you like a stick of rock, then you have the gravitas to cope with anything.

Substance Before Style

I love the story of Max Planck (the Nobel Prize-winning physicist), the lecture tour and the chauffeur.[6] Having won the prize in 1918, Planck was invited to speak all over Germany. Each time he gave the same talk on quantum mechanics. By the time he'd heard it a few times, the chauffeur had learnt the talk off by heart.

Lightheartedly the chauffeur suggested that he and the professor swap roles (Shakespeare would have approved of this plot): the chauffeur would give the talk and the professor would sit in the audience wearing the driver's uniform. That night the chauffeur gave the talk while the professor watched. All went swimmingly until the time came for questions. A fellow physicist asked a tricky question. The driver, stymied, replied, 'What a simple question, beneath the standards of a great city like Munich. My chauffeur can answer it!'

The chauffeur could get away with polished delivery having learnt the speech like an actor. But like an actor he didn't have gravitas because there was no depth – something that caught him out when questioned (despite the quick-thinking response!). He'd learnt to mimic the style but he lacked the substance – the 'bottom' as Major-General Shaw described it, using the Yorkshire expression which means: 'A body of stories back there. You know that that gravitas comes from somewhere, comes from a depth of experience and knowledge.'

Be aware that gravitas exists purely in your zone of expertise. It's important to understand the limits of that zone. It takes at least 10,000 hours to learn the knowledge part of the gravitas equation, as wisdom and expertise take time, experience and repetition to acquire.[7]

Step out of your zone of experience and your gravitas will vanish like Cinderella's carriage. You need to know the point at which you get out of your depth – and not be too shy to say so. Your wisdom is the source of your stability, your ballast. You need to be attuned to how far you can go to the edges of your knowledge before you become unstable. Of course, you should keep extending your zone of knowledge.

Earn your stripes, learn to sound authoritative and then, and only then, will others truly trust you to fly the plane. Since earning your stripes is up to you, sounding authoritative is where we're going next.

Good Speech is Deceptive

Speech is easier to lose the thread of … voiced thoughts have to be clearer than written ones if they are to sound coherent and spontaneous. They have to emerge from a background of extensive reflection and focus. There's no room for waffle like there is on the page. In short, speaking well sounds easy and isn't.

ALAIN DE BOTTON, PHILOSOPHER, WRITER AND BROADCASTER

Speech, as Alain de Botton points out, is a deceptive little beast. Those who make it sound easy, conversational and concise have often done a lot of thinking behind the scenes. They have no need to waffle because their thoughts are clear. They have no need to fill silence with ums and other verbal fillers because they trust their thinking. So, how, once you've done the thinking and sifting and reflecting that we've just explored, do you cut the fillers and speak clearly?

You create a cast-iron structure with clear links and signposts, that's how. It's an absolute essential of gravitas. When you get good at it you can even learn to do it on the hoof. And if you want to know how to structure and present an argument in a formal environment, ask a judge.

Judges spend a lot of time listening to people speak. Articulate, authoritative, anxious – they hear it all. And they know what does and doesn't work when it comes to presenting your thoughts with gravitas in a formal situation. So I went to an appeals court judge and asked what the secret was to speaking with gravitas. The answer came back clear, you have to be able to distil the argument down to the essence:

Be very clear … what your points are – clarity of expression is everything. Clarity, simplicity of language, the right word, the right expression – in easy-to-understand terms. Put your own template with clarity and intellectual honesty.

Though this may sound challenging, there are some simple structures that you can use to help you.

Try This: The News Reporter Structure

Everything that can be thought can be thought clearly.
Everything that can be put into words can be put clearly.
LUDWIG WITTGENSTEIN, PHILOSOPHER

Out of intense complexities, intense simplicities emerge.
WINSTON CHURCHILL, PRIME MINISTER

Here's a clear, simple structure that you can use to speak with authority. I learnt it working with news reporters and if it works when you're standing outside the Houses of Parliament with a news producer shouting into your earpiece from a stressed-out gallery, you can guarantee that it's been crash-tested.

To create your structure, follow the instructions below and think through each point in turn. You'll need a pen and paper or a computer.

What's Your Angle?

First, choose your focus. The speech-writer and *The Times* columnist Philip Collins explains:[8]

> You need to be entirely clear in a sentence or two what you are saying. 'What's the topic?' does not mean 'What is the subject?' It means what do *you* have to say about it?

Journalists call this your *angle*. It's key to originality and to interest because it allows you to focus. You can't cover the whole subject so choose a specific aspect, a particular take, and focus there. Choose an aspect that interests you. Your point of view as they say in movies. Your focus. The reason that people want to come and hear you speak. Your take on life. Don't be bland. As Collins says, if no one could disagree with you on your angle it's not yet interesting enough. Take a stand and you find something interesting to explore.

Headlines, Main Story, Wrap

Now organise your points into a clear structure. It's like a news bulletin: headlines, main stories, summing up. It works for a five-minute introduction or a conference speech. Like news, it helps to get the big rocks in first. News reporters will tell you to always have two points and a spare. You start with the most important point, then the second most important point and you know you can drop the third if needs be. You *always* go to the wrap because summing up is key to help the audience remember.

- **Headlines** Tell the audience what you're going to tell them. Explain what you're going to talk about and give it context and background – a frame. Signpost the key points you'll be focusing on.
- **Point 1** Get your biggest point in first.
- **Point 2** Then your second biggest point.
- **Point 3** Then your third (as this is the least important point, you can always cut it if time dictates).
- **Wrap** Sum up. Tell the audience what you've told them – with a twist, a question, a new perspective so that they get a summing up and a new idea.

We will come back to this structure in Presentations in Part Two.

Short is Good

We need only ensure that our speech is not diffuse and wandering, that it does not stop in the middle and does not run on too far, and that it is separated by clauses and has well-rounded, complete sentences.

CICERO, ROMAN STATESMAN, ORATOR AND WRITER

Once you've got a clear structure the next step to gravitas is to understand how good speech works.

There's a great secret to speaking well. You can take a good guess at what it is by looking at poetry, song lyrics and even nursery rhymes – but not prose. Short sentences, separated by a pause – *good*. Long sentences that run together and make you out of breath – *bad*.

Each day *Today* presenter Simon Jack comes face to face with business leaders under pressure. He's clear on what makes some stand out head and shoulders above the rest.

> Talking slowly, in reasonably short sentences, without a million subclauses is the sign of someone who knows what they're saying; it shows that you have a very ordered, uncluttered mind – you're in command of your brief.

Brevity is crucial, the soul of wit. Or if you prefer Dorothy Parker, the soul of ... lingerie. Short is good. Short words. Short lines. Short speeches. What you want in speech is 'good hard clear meanings' says Peggy Noonan. Short words give you that clarity, 'They are like pickets in a fence, slim and unimpressive on their own but sturdy and effective when strung together.'[9] Short sentences are brilliant for you because they're easy to say. They're even better for your listeners because they can actually take in what you're saying to them. Perfect.

Once you have grasped the importance of short sentences you will notice good speakers using them. Start looking for them, start listening to them and start using them yourself. It will transform how you communicate.

Phrases Good, Paragraphs Bad

> *Phrasing: A clear perception of the formal division ...*
> *into well-defined sentences and their parts; secondly, as*
> *referring to the right method of marking those divisions so that ...*
> *they may be evident to the hearer; and, thirdly, as referring*
> *to the correct and expressive rendering of each division.*
> J. ALFRED JOHNSTONE, *TOUCH PHRASING AND INTERPRETATION*

Winston Churchill hated paragraphs, preferring short lines and dashes in his speeches as they were easier to bring to life. Sending back paragraph-filled speeches for rewriting, Churchill would badger his secretaries saying that a speech is blank verse, not an essay, and that a speech without dashes is a magazine article, not a speech.

What you need for good speech is the instinct of the poet or song-writer for short, neat lines. It's what Cicero called speaking in 'nearly verses' – short lines as you see in poetry. It sounds so simple, but it will *transform* your gravitas and make you measured when you speak. The cognitive psychologist Paul Fraisse questioned whether a three to six-second time period might be central to the human brain.[10] When you think that the timing of an in- and out-breath, a typical musical phrase, a line of a song, a line of poetry and a normal utterance all last two to seven seconds, it makes sense that we might want to use the same phrasing to speak with. And in a Twitter age these short, clear ideas are more important than ever.

Journalist and presenter Jon Snow talked to me about how he puts his own phrasing on a news script that has been written for him:

> You can even do quite a lot by just re-punctuating it. I might put a dash in to slow up for a moment. Or some dots. I'll often change a full stop into something which has a continuum … don't go away yet because there's another thought here.

In speech I'd advise you to do the same. When you get to the end of a sentence give yourself an audible full stop. In a long sentence have an audible comma. That way you stay in control of the thinking and don't become a runaway train.

We understand this principle when it comes to food. We know that if we try to eat something too big in one go we will choke. Sentences that are too long have a similar effect on the brains of your audience – they become indigestible. As you cut your pizza into slices, you must measure out your speech into bite-sized pieces. Studies have even shown that if you chunk the information into bite-sized sections the audience see you as more intelligent – because they've had time to think about what you're saying.

Try This: Speak in Verse, Not in Prose

The shorter words ... appeal with greater force.
WINSTON CHURCHILL, PRIME MINISTER

Here are the rules:

1. Short words are better than long words.
2. Short punchy sentences are better than long ones.
3. Short 'verses' are better than long rambling paragraphs.

Below are a few lines from one of Churchill's most famous speeches. I've laid them out in two ways.

Version One (Whole Pizza)

Read the text below in a rush, without stopping and notice how it makes you feel breathless and like a runaway train.

> We shall fight on the beaches – We shall fight on the landing grounds. We shall fight in the fields and in the streets – We shall fight in the hills – We shall never surrender.

Version Two (Bite-sized)

Now read these lines aloud and take a small pause at the dash or the line end so you have a moment to breathe and can think one thought at a time with the audience. Notice how you feel in control, as if the train stops at each station and the passengers have the chance to enjoy the scenery.

We shall fight on the beaches [breath]
We shall fight on the landing grounds [breath]
We shall fight in the fields and in the streets [breath]
We shall fight in the hills [longer in-breath]
We shall never surrender.

Did you notice that this version allowed you to speak at a natural conversational pace? And that the words have more colour and connection because you've taken a little bit of time to live them?

The Art of Pre-planned Spontaneity

The magic happens when you memorise your pieces
to the point where you no longer have to think about them.
If you're still thinking about it on stage then it's not real –
it needs to be in your system so you can give it the space.

INDIGO WILLIAMS, PERFORMANCE POET

Sometimes to be less eloquent is actually to be more eloquent. It helps to loosen things up a little. It's a bit like the skill of dressing for smart-casual events. The aim is to look both uber-relaxed and uber-elegant. Good speech is similar. What you need to know to achieve conversational elegance is to know how to do pre-planned spontaneity. It takes a little work but it's worth it because you seem like a natural.

The main rule is to learn the bones of the ideas so you can relax and take the audience on a journey. 'Memory is genius – but you have to do something with it,' said the poet Robert Lowell.[11] When you know your words by heart, you speak from the heart. When you speak from the heart, people hang on your every word. It's a no-brainer. If you want to be the effortless, authentic, enthusiastic speaker who makes it look easy *you have to know it well enough to go script-free.*

Yes, that's right, step away from the script. If you have a script the message you're sending people is 'I don't know what I'm talking about really, so I had to write it down'. Far, far cooler to say something short (and seemingly off the cuff – but *not*) and do it without notes. People will be impressed and you will be remembered. What we're talking about here is pre-planned spontaneity, the secret skill of anyone with gravitas. When the content is there and the structure is clear in your mind you can have a relaxed chat. You let the words come because you know what you're talking about. That's the sign of the expert and it really enhances gravitas.

Why? It's about working memory and the space it takes up in your brain. If you have to work to remember your words, you're in trouble. If your working memory is straining to retrieve information, then you can't think. There's no room. And if you can't think then your gravitas is in trouble. So there's no two ways about it, you need to learn your words and show up with your content clear in your mind not on a piece of paper (or on slides). There are times when you may have to give a very formal speech, for example if reporters are writing down your every word, at these times a script is acceptable. But in less formal moments even a long speech, with practice, can be delivered from memory.

I've done closing plenary speeches at conferences without notes and I've used the strategy I'm going to show you below. You have to get the argument clear, of course, cook the speech down to bullet points and examples, then practise and practise until you can tell it like a story at dinner. That is the art of a great speech in the modern age. It takes work, but it's worth it. If you show up and read a speech verbatim the audience don't get you, they get a typescript. It's you they want or you might as well have just emailed the script.

If the length of the speech worries you, remember you can always add more Q and As – which people often enjoy more – and cut the length of the speech.

Try This: How to be a Natural Speaker

The first thing I should say is that there is no such thing as a natural speaker. You just have to know the shortcuts. To make speaking look easy you need to do a little strategic preparation. The work it takes is well worth it. Like most things that seem effortless, it takes work behind the scenes to have the pay-off of compelling ease in front of your audience. You can prepare in a light way, make it fun. Just do it though. Please.

1. Distil and work out your signposts – the key points on your journey.
2. Practise the links so you can go smoothly from point to point.
3. Get it conversational and relaxed, 'in the muscle' as actors call it. It means that you know it in the body as much as the mind – you know your subject so well that the words are there at your fingertips.

1. Distil
These tips for distilling content come from Peter Everett, a senior radio producer at BBC Radio 4.

- Write down bullet points for the ideas you want to get across.
- Then condense them. Boil them down to just one word. Mental triggers you can pull up when required.

- That list of around six words gives you half an hour of a presentation.

2. Find the Links

Then it's about segues. Once you have those six or so words then it's a lot about making the links clear. If you know your links it feels great to move between them. You can be relaxed and deliberate about the journey of your content. Good links come from the connection in your mind between ideas. As Peggy Noonan suggests, 'Where you falter, alter.' If it's not clear in your mind when you rehearse you'll be in trouble in front of an audience. Get the links crystal clear and presentation becomes as easy as conversation.

Since the links are what make a good presentation, practising matters. Practise moving smoothly between ideas. Record yourself practising. How do you get conversationally from one point to another? Simplify and clarify your links so that they take you neatly from point to point.

With the links clear in your mind, you can be relaxed and conversational. As Peter Everett explains:

> If you start to worry that with only six words you might lose your thread in the conversation. We're used to talking to people who pause, who go back on themselves, who repeat themselves and think about things while they're talking. We don't mind that. It sounds right.

3. Learn by Heart

Ordinary things slip easily from the memory while the striking and the novel stay longer in the mind.
RHETORICA AD HERENNIUM

The only good way to learn something is to practise it. Practice makes you good. Psychologists and coaches will tell you that practice creates familiarity and familiarity makes you feel safer, which then helps reduce feelings of anxiety. Once you have a simple structure (see above) practice becomes more fun anyway because you can be conversational.

KC Baker calls this the 'bones'.[12] Think of a skeleton. You need to understand how the skeleton fits together – the knee bone's connected to the thigh bone and so on. With your speech, what comes first? What's the key image? Then what's the next key idea? What's the link between the first and second idea?

Write them on a card. Test your memory. Put the card where you can't see it. Run your words. Notice the points where you get stuck and change them until they flow and you can speak them easily. Check your card to see if you got them right. If you missed anything spend more time getting that segue really smooth in your mind.

Drawing pictures of key symbols and signposts in the talk can also help if you're a visual person. For example, if you had to talk about a team you might draw a group of people. If profits are up an arrow pointing up or a pound sign will remind you. They are triggers for the memory. They really help you relax and get the content off by heart.

If the words you have planned don't work when you say them change them, so that they flow smoothly from your brain to your mouth to the ears of the audience.

That way you look natural, the fine art of pre-planned spontaneity. Then you have thinking space to react in the moment. You feel more confident, you speak with more authority and you have more gravitas. Result.

Memory House

Creating a memory house is an ancient method that is still used by memory champions today. To do it Cicero says that you 'Form mental images of the facts you wish to remember, and store those images in the localities.' Simply create a house in your mind's eye – your own is often easiest. Then choose a key image for each main idea in your content. Visualise walking around the house room by room. Place the images of the ideas in the order you want to speak them, one in each room. For example, if you are talking about last year's results you might visualise a really successful project, perhaps a product or the launch event. See it clearly with lots of colour and the picture crystal clear in your mind.

Then to remember what you have to say you visualise walking around each room in turn. You can do this in your mind's eye if you're travelling home from work.

Or you can even do it for real. Walk around your house room by room as you speak each idea. Moving around helps get the words in the muscle, which means you know it so well it's dropped deep into the memory, it's not hogging up your working memory anymore.

Principle 3: Find Your Voice Toolkit

Be Concise and Clear

George Orwell's rules to help writers find the clarity of their voice are just as relevant for finding your gravitas:[13]

- Never use a long word where a short one will do.
- If it is possible to cut a word out, always cut it out.
- Never use a foreign phrase, a scientific word or a jargon word if you can think of an everyday English equivalent.
- Break any of these rules sooner than say anything outright barbarous.

Expand Your Vocabulary

Read and listen voraciously. Learn new languages and learn new words in your own language. When you see a word you don't know find out what it means and how to say it and use it.

Listen

We learn new words best when we hear them and then speak them. This is a good sequence to follow when you want to become more articulate. Listen to great words – whether you go to the theatre or listen to the radio or talking books. Bring some of that richness into your own speaking and writing.

Short Words

Short words are powerful in speech. Use them with pride and eliminate jargon.

Speak in Short Sentences

Keep your sentences short and concise. Think about poems as a guide. To avoid rambling when you come to the end of a thought, you can always close your mouth and breathe.

Practice is Key to Overcoming Anxiety

If you can really practise until you are just on the edge of comfortable with an almost pleasant frisson of nerves, you're ready for a good delivery. The main thing is to get the bones, the segues clear in your mind, and practise enough that your working memory is freed up and you can be relaxed, yourself and attentive to the audience. Once you've had the feeling of being conversational and in control, you will get addicted to the thrill of doing it and to the great results and positive response from the audience.

Principle 4:
Speak So Others Listen

How to Speak with Impact, Authority and Power

Why on earth people who have something to say that is worth
hearing, should not take the trouble to learn how to make it heard,
is one of the strange mysteries of modern life … Their methods are
as reasonable as to try to pour some precious stuff … through a
non-conducting pipe, which could … be opened.

ARTHUR CONAN DOYLE, *THE LOST WORLD*

Winston Churchill saw the ability to speak powerfully and persuasively as the most important of all the talents, saying that the art of speech 'wields a power more durable than that of a great king' because it made one 'an independent force in the world. Abandoned by his party, betrayed by his friends, stripped of his offices. Whoever can command this power is still formidable.'[1]

Research agrees. In 1998 psychology lecturer Stephen Ceci set out to test this voice power.[2] Each term he taught a developmental psychology course to 300 students. Intrigued about the power of his voice to make impact he decided to do an experiment. He would teach exactly the same content twice, once in the fall term and once in spring. In the vacation between the terms he trained with a professional voice coach. When students were asked to rate the spring semester class the ratings for Ceci's teaching went through the roof. Students were far more positive about Ceci's knowledge as a teacher, his organisation and his openness, even though the content that had been delivered was identical. And even the students' results improved.

If you'd like to have this voice power you're in the right place. We'll think about the fundamentals of great speech and you'll find that it's easier than you think to get the voice you want.

The Gravitas Boosters: Tone, Pause and Pace

No one in education ever mentioned public speaking.
It was decades before anyone told me to pause and look the
audience in the eye or not move around so much. All of that
belonged to stuff you might need for the school play, not for life.
As ever, there's a big hole in the education system.

ALAIN DE BOTTON, PHILOSOPHER, WRITER AND BROADCASTER

A University of Michigan study in 2011 looked into how aspects of speech influence decisions on the telephone.[3] Researchers found that there were certain characteristics that made a marked difference. What mattered were tone, pause and pace, aspects of speech that Cicero was waxing lyrical about thousands of years earlier.

Low tone mattered. The most influential speakers had low vocal tone and weren't overly animated (it can sound a bit unnatural – think of those bright 'Have a nice day' greetings). Low, relaxed (rather than forced down) voices helped men in particular make impact on their listeners. What surprised the researchers was that tonal variety (the music of the voice) didn't make too much difference.

Pauses mattered most of all. In the University of Michigan research the most influential speakers paused regularly and naturally. Those who paused naturally – i.e. they paused at natural ends of thoughts – were the most effective. The more you use short sentences, the easier it is to pause. We're going to think about how using *phrasing* and *space between phrases* can help you really make an impact when you speak.

Pace was also key. Influential speakers found the perfect balance of pace, neither too fast nor too slow. Those who spoke moderately fast were more successful at getting others to agree than those who spoke very fast or very slow. People get pace wrong because they think talking slowly makes them sound less than bright. The key refinement when you talk slowly is that you must do it with energy. A slow pace must have power in the voice and energy, then it is dynamic *and* easy to understand – a double whammy. We're going to think about how the *weight* of your emphasis on the right words – the rhythm of your speech – can help you find the right pace.

How to Get the Voice Tone You Want

A slightly lower register always comes across as having
authority. Emphasis is very important and you've got to have
modulation in your voice. That makes people sit up and listen.
This person is telling me something I need to know.
SIMON JACK, BUSINESS AND ECONOMICS PRESENTER, *TODAY*, BBC RADIO 4

When I started at drama school I had a thin voice. I felt very insecure about it. These days I draw real confidence from the knowledge that I have a much more resonant, powerful voice. I know – from experience – that it's possible for all of us to improve our voices.

Finding a good voice is well worth it. Research shows a deep, relaxed voice has the power to help you – whether you want to win an election or attract the object of your desire. It's all about ease. A good voice is not forced – it flows. A good voice is a hot-water bottle for the soul because it comes from the absolute centre of who you are.

The Greek orator Demosthenes proves the power of practice. He went from being called The Stammerer – the poor lad couldn't even pronounce the 'r' of 'rhetoric' – to being known as a great speaker and as Plutarch, the Greek historian, biographer and essayist, said, 'One who owed all the power and ability he had in speaking to labour and industry.' Industry indeed. He built an underground study and practised until he was the toast of the town. He had the self-belief to change the habit and work the muscle.

I want you to have the same belief that you can change. Maybe you notice the power source of your voice when you sing or laugh. It's the power in your gut. It's the voice that comes from your torso rather than your throat. It's the free, energetic, honest voice you speak with when you're two before the bad habits of adulthood – slumping, poor breathing, tiredness, rushing, anxiety – get in the way.

Try This 1: Find Your Diaphragm

Phrenos or phren was the Greek word for diaphragm (our modern word descends from *phrenos*). What's interesting is that the word *phrenos* encompassed a lot more than our modern definition of diaphragm. For the Greeks *phrenos* actually meant mind, heart and diaphragm. As they saw it the diaphragm united all our expression. My belief is that they were right. Your diaphragm is your gravitas and voice secret weapon. Most people don't know very much about it so those in the know have a definite gravitas and presence advantage.

So, what does it look like? It cuts your torso in half so it looks like a mixture of parachute and hat! Doming up into the ribs it essentially cuts the body in half. Above it is air, the lungs, the voice and the heart. Below it are the liver, spleen, stomach, intestines and kidneys.

Like your heart and lungs the diaphragm moves continuously. As you breathe in it descends, pushing the stomach out as the organs move down. It's a brilliant, natural inner massage if you use it well. The diaphragm works like a pump and the more it moves the more effectively it pumps air around the system. The bonus is that its effective pumping action also assists the heart.

1. Take your thumb and place it just below where your ribs separate (just below where the front of a bra strap goes). Underneath a layer of muscle you get a feel for where the diaphragm attaches at the front. Give it a gentle massage and feel it soften.

2. Gently tap that point and speak or let out a big belly laugh or a loud yawn. Feel your voice drop out low and easy – a big easy of a sound. That's your natural, free voice. Your birthright. And it's a big source of gravitas.

3. Another exercise is to jump up and down on the spot and speak. Feel that your voice comes from deep down at the centre of you, almost from your spine. That's a diaphragmatic sound. You already have that voice – you just need to release it.

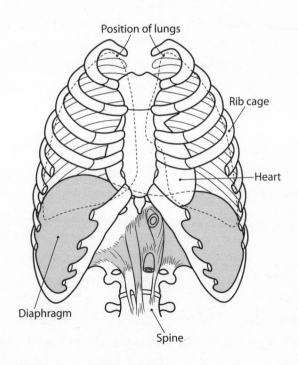

Try This 2: Sing

Singing helps you access the freedom of your natural voice. Notice how your voice travels from deep in your body. Then speak the same words you just sang. Play between singing and speaking until you can speak and sing from the same point – your chest and stomach, not your throat. Yawning or chanting works well for this too. Singing a speech or presentation when no one's around is a great way to get your voice projecting and powerful.

Try This 3: Head, Heart or Gut?

If you want real vocal expression it's best to play with where you *feel* your voice, rather than hear it. We never hear our own voice properly (blame the ear canal for that).

There are three main places to feel your voice – head, heart and gut. High notes resonate high in the head, mid notes in the heart and low notes in the gut.

- **Head voice** is intellect, thoughtfulness, curiosity (Bill Gates, Christine Lagarde).
- **Heart voice** is love, passion, care, empathy, warmth (Desmond Tutu, Oprah Winfrey).
- **Gut voice** is power, drive, action (Margaret Thatcher, Malcolm X).

Find Your Three Voices

1. **Head** Think of something that takes you into an analytical place – into your head. Say the days of the week. Feel the voice in your head.

2. **Heart** Put a hand on your heart and think of someone you love. Say the days of the week.

3. **Gut** Tap your stomach then perform a physical movement that has power (punching, stamping, gesturing vehemently, etc.). Say the days of the week.

Do you notice that each of the three voices has a different quality? You can speak from the head, feeling and sounding objective and in control. Or you can channel energy through the heart and chest, feeling and emanating warmth and compassion. Or you can find your gut voice with its power and commitment, driving change.

They are vocal gears to help you adjust to the needs of others and the situation you find yourself in. And of course you can mix them up too.

Breathe In Emotions

You can also change your voice tone simply by choosing a different emotion. Use your smartphone or a voice recorder and try out this exercise. You'll notice differences in the tone simply because you've breathed in different emotions.

1. Think of a moment in your life where you've felt incredible happiness. Let that memory be breathed in, letting the breath arrive as a reflex in its own time. Notice the feeling you get in your diaphragm on the in-breath. Then speak on the out-breath. Notice your voice is warm and comes from the heart. It resonates differently because of the emotion.

2. Now do the same with curiosity or any other emotion that comes to mind. If you breathe in the emotion it will change your voice on the way out.

The Power of the Pause

Pauses strengthen the voice. They also render
thoughts more clear-cut by separating them.

RHETORICA AD HERENNIUM

I want you to learn to love pauses. Not rushed or panicky pauses. No one could love those. I want you to learn to love pregnant pauses. Pauses full of ease, life, breath and thought. Pauses that move your thinking on, which give you inspiration. Pauses that are, to echo the old Coca-Cola slogan, the 'pause that refreshes'.

The ability to be comfortable with a pause is central to gravitas. It says that you trust yourself; that you're not desperate to please or to fill a silence. In a moment of silence you understand the truth of the old acting rule that the most powerful person in the room has the most relaxed breathing pattern (no matter what their job title).

Pauses are also persuasive. In the University of Michigan research (see page 86), which looked at what made for effective telephone sales, pauses made the biggest difference of all. As ever, balance was key in the best communication. When it came to pauses neither too much, nor too little, but just enough was required for effective influence.

Too little pausing didn't work at all. Those who paused naturally, 3.5 times a minute, were the most successful at influencing their audience. People who paused too much were seen as stilted and uncomfortable – 'dis-fluent'. But it was interesting that even the most dis-fluent interviewers had higher success rates than those who were too perfect. Not pausing at all was the worst. It sounded fake and listeners didn't trust or warm to the speaker so there was no sale.

So, how do you learn to pause? Let's debunk the myths.

Myth 1 Pauses make me sound like I don't know what I'm talking about.

No A relaxed pause gives you ease and conversational elegance. Sure, you have to be prepared and fluent, practised. Once you are, then it's best to let each thought land, give it space and your audience time to process it. When you give an audience time to think, research shows they perceive you as more intelligent because they have had a chance to catch up with you and think about what you're saying.

Myth 2 Pauses will slow me down and bore the audience.

No What's really boring for an audience is when a speaker gallops through their content because they don't want to waste the audience's time. If they go too fast the audience can't keep up so they stop listening and that's when it all gets truly boring. It's far better to deliver each line with weight and emphasis and lead your audience thought by thought, so they hear every idea clearly and remember what you say.

Myth 3 If I pause I might lose my thread.

No If you think of the pause as a permitted, in fact essential, *breathing space* and consciously give yourself permission to pause and *breathe* then you are oxygenating your brain. If you can pause and oxygenate your brain, and you have a plan, then you will be fine because you will be relaxed and prepared. If you pause and hold your breath, then yes, you might not feel entirely confident to continue. When you panic and stop breathing your brain is deprived of oxygen. It does take a little practice to master pausing and phrasing. See page 95 for how to do it.

Pauses are good. To master them you have to find the balance. Not pausing at all sounds scripted and fake; pausing too much sounds jerky and uncomfortable. What works best is a relaxed pause that reveals clear thinking underneath. Then you can enjoy a totally natural pause in which you relax and think of the next thought, rather than rushing to fill silence.

To understand pauses you also need to understand phrasing. That's what we're moving on to next.

Pausing and Phrasing

Everything I say is the result of thought / Every thought I have needs a breath / Breathing is also known as inspiration / Therefore I inspire the thought with breath / Which in turn becomes sound / And with articulation becomes speech / Then I can turn the speech into words / In order to share with the audience my original thought.

ROYAL ACADEMY OF DRAMATIC ART (LONDON) ADVICE

Phrases and pauses are a blissful combination for an audience. They create neat, bite-sized chunks of meaning that allow your audience to digest what you have to say, moment by moment, thought by thought. A good phrase is made more marvellous by a well-timed pause.

Phrases are the antidote to the sin of *plonking*. To understand plonking think of a child learning to play the piano and plonking through, note by note, versus a great musician who plays phrase by phrase, each section having its own meaning and unity.

The word plonking actually comes from radio. It describes what bad announcers do – speaking word by word with occasional emphasis to show they are still awake. But because they're going word by word the meaning doesn't come through.

Try This 1: How to Combine Pausing and Phrasing

*The fermata is a mark from the composer to the conductor –
'Hold the pause for as long as you like.' But when we finally
have the attention of an audience our instinct is to rush.
'Please don't stare, okay, I'm hurrying, there, I'm done.'
It doesn't work that way. Attention is precious. If you've
got something to say, say it. Slowly, with effect.*

SETH GODIN, MARKETER AND AUTHOR

1. Find a poem you like, a nursery rhyme will do.
2. Mark breath marks at the ends of the lines like this:
   Line one: Mary had a little lamb//
   Line two: Its fleece was white as snow//
   Etc.
3. Now say the poem out load. Speak a line *then close your mouth*.
4. Read the next line. *Close your mouth*.
5. Try this exercise in front of a mirror. Say something then watch your mouth close, wait for the breath in and when it comes imagine breathing in a lovely smell, so you are relaxed and easy in the breathing.

Try This 2: In Conversation – How to Use Pausing and Phrasing in Speech

Now try the pausing and phrasing technique with something you might have to say for real, such as introducing yourself to a meeting perhaps. We all do totally natural pauses when we chat. Where we struggle is when we're under pressure – the very moments where we need to make a great impression.

In speech keep your phrasing clear. Speak in bite-sized phrases and separate them with a little pause. If you don't want to be interrupted the trick is to make a subtle gesture just as you pause and to hold it through the pause. That way people know there's more to come.

The key is to keep the phrasing and pausing going and not rush off like a runaway train. Take time to stop at each station and think each thought with your audience.

So you have to practise. Keep the tiny pause at the end of each sentence. It's imperceptible to others because they're thinking about what you just said and it gives you time to gather your thoughts. What feels to you like an age an audience simply won't notice. They'll be too busy listening.

Pace

A good pace is what you would naturally say to one person. If you're rattling like a machine gun one person is not going to be very interested. There are stories that annoy, upset, amuse, and in some senses I'm hoping that the viewer will also be amused, annoyed, upset or horrified.

JON SNOW, JOURNALIST AND PRESENTER

The third gravitas booster is pace. Pace must be intertwined with meaning and the needs of the audience. The best pace allows you to connect with the meaning of every word as you speak it at exactly the right pace for your audience to take it in.

Pace is like the three bears' porridge; you want it just right. Goldilocks found the porridge 'too hot' and 'too cold'. Pace is best when *it's not too fast or too slow*. The only way to ascertain *just right* in pace terms is to be tuned in to what the audience needs (that's why getting content in the muscle matters so much).

Alice in Wonderland refuses to talk to the Cheshire Cat until she can see both his ears. With audiences you need to wait for the eyes. You can see people thinking – their eyes move as they process. If the content is new to the audience you need to start where they are and take each idea slowly. Give them time to take in the idea before you move on. If they are old hands you can probably afford to pick up the pace, but you need to notice if their eyes are bright and focused or dull and confused. Shining eyes tell you the pace is right. Dull eyes tell you to adjust. If in doubt ask a question. You'll soon find out what they need.

Too fast means running ahead of yourself, blurting out sentences and tripping over words whether out of excitement or anxiety. Too fast is usually risky. I admit that sometimes it can communicate passion if used in short bursts with control but usually it confuses people. They can't keep up with you or it worries them. They see and hear you rushing and worry that you might be feeling nervous or trying to hide something.

You know when the pace is too fast because you are skipping ahead of the ideas, usually out of nerves. You see the audience's eyes go dead because they can't keep up. If you realise you're rushing take a moment. Breathe. Ask a question. Then consciously put the brakes on. Go one thought at a time, like a train stopping at each station. Take a look at the scenery rather than rushing ahead like the brakes don't work.

Too slow worries the audience just as much but for different reasons. They worry that perhaps you aren't thinking fast enough. They get anxious for you – is your slowness because you are stressed or tired and becoming distracted? Or maybe you needed more time to get the content in the muscle, so you're working hard to remember what to say next?

You know you're too slow because you get interruptions, people try to finish your sentence or they look bored. You might see frustration in their faces or them looking at their phone. Or – the signs that every performer dreads – they fidget or cough. Coughs are a bad sign. When you notice these dreaded signs pick up the pace pronto. Keep the energy up and match the pace to the thinking.

Interestingly in the University of Michigan research (see page 86) the sweet spot for pace when it came to influencing an audience was a rate of about 3.5 words per second. It might be a good experiment to time your words per minute but I wouldn't obsess about it. The shining eyes of an audience is a better marker.

Listen to pace in the world. Who compels you because their pace is just right? Who frustrates or confuses you because they are too fast? Who annoys or bores you because they are too slow? Learn what to do or, equally powerfully, what not to do from these examples and become a connoisseur of pace.

Make Words Work

Speak clearly if you speak at all,
carve every word before you let it fall.
OLIVER WENDELL HOLMES, PHYSICIAN AND POET

In *Alice's Adventures in Wonderland* Humpty Dumpty says to Alice, 'When I make a word do a lot of work, I pay it extra.' Working your words is a gravitas essential. We're going to think about weight and space to help you do just that.

Weight is the way you use emphasis, space is the way you pause. When you understand how they can help you your speech will transform.

In English certain words matter more than others and so they get more stress (which is more breath power in speech). You can see it when the voice is recorded. If you get a chance look at the sound waves as your voice is recorded and see the lines rise on the emphasised words to indicate more breath coming through your larynx. It's why a sound engineer can usually see where you are in a sentence from the sound waves.

What *really makes* a *difference* is to *know* which *words* to *stress* in a *sentence*. Often people just string words together without any sense of the key meaning words. Gravitas in speech means using emphasis to give certain words weight. Think of what happens when someone learning English gets the stresses wrong. Although the vocabulary is correct it's incredibly difficult to understand. 'Hello *my* name *is* Caroline' is hard to understand because it's not what we expect.

Think about saying your name to an audience at the start of a talk or meeting. If you say, 'Hellomynameiscarolinegoyder,' rushing through it, it doesn't express your authority or your belief in the value of the message.

If you say, '*Hello*. My name is *Caroline Goyder*' as a newsreader says, 'Here is the *news*' then you start to sound like you're saying it like you mean it and like you have a right to be there. It has gravitas.

These emphasised words are what were once called telegram words. Think about an old-fashioned telegram. Only the absolutely essential words for meaning are communicated as each word costs money. The whole purpose of selecting these words is to telegraph to the listener that these are the words to pay attention to. It's the highlighter pen of good speech.

Try This: Power Words

1. Mark the Power Words

Choose a poem or piece of prose and underline the important words in pencil. Not all words are equally important. In the following sentence I've underlined the key words:

The <u>words</u> that <u>matter</u> are the <u>meaning words.</u>

The meaning words are usually the *nouns* and *verbs* and sometimes *adjectives*. When you obey the underlying heartbeat of the language you are easier to listen to.

2. Find the Stress

You may remember mention at school of a specific rhythm in Shakespeare's verse:

To *be* or *not to be, that* is the *question.*

Sentences in normal speech have a similar heartbeat (though of course we don't speak in poetry so the rhythm's not as regular). So when you speak to an audience make sure that those meaning words get more air pressure – give them a bit of welly!

In speech it helps to feel that rhythm supporting you. Point up the important words. Gesturing as you say them is a good way to practise. If you record yourself doing this you will hear a *real* difference. The main thing to notice is that the rhythm runs all the way through a phrase whether you're saying 'To *be* or *not* to *be, that* is the *question*' or '*Hello*. My name is *Caroline Goyder.*' It helps to feel the rhythm subtly underneath the words. Keep the energy going through the phrase to give a feeling of conviction.

3. Emphasise the Meaning Words

Once you understand how stress and the telegram words work, then it helps to understand emphasis. Where stress is the underlying rhythm of a language – the heartbeat – emphasis is the word or words you pick out of a phrase to highlight meaning. Actors will tell you that you only emphasise one word in each line. Most of the time we do this unconsciously, but being aware of it can really boost your artistry in front of an audience. It's the difference between saying, 'I never eat meat' and 'I *never* eat meat.' It gives a different prominence and power to the thought. It can also change the meaning. For example, if someone says, 'He *says* she didn't break it' you know to be suspicious.

Emphasis also highlights new ideas. For example, if you want to move from one section to another in a meeting or presentation you might say, 'So, we've thought about what happened last year, now let's focus on the *future*.' You give the new subject a bit of extra power as you say it so that people know what's coming and really pay attention. It's a powerful auditory signpost to hook information on and it makes you memorable.

4. Drive the Thought Through to the End

As directors tell actors, make sure you drive the thought through to the end of the line. The mistake people make is to start thinking about the next line before they've finished the words they're speaking. The result is that their energy tails off and their voice dies away. It makes them sound uncertain and unconvincing. What you have to do instead is really stay in the words you're speaking and give the last word a punch, like a tennis player giving the ball a little topspin. It can help to gesture on that last word as it drives the power of the voice.

5. Speak Clearly

We've thought about space in terms of pausing when you speak, but the other aspect of space to think about is the space you need to create in your mouth when you speak. If there's no space and your jaw, tongue and lips don't really move then the sound just runs together. People find it hard to hear what you say.

The art is to create subtle muscularity, as actors call it, by using the muscles of speech fully and shaping the words clearly and with conviction (imagine you're speaking to an ever-so-slightly hard of hearing person, who you really want to communicate an idea to). This is not about taaaalking sloooowly or too self-consciously, which makes most people sound a little strange. It's about really using every word because you care about communicating it, making it work for you fully, not throwing anything away, not muttering, not rushing so you trip over words. Just take each word in its own good time and use it fully. In other words it's not about you sounding good, it's about the communication of an idea. It's about being mindful of your speech. So as you create space between words, create space to shape the words fully.

Speaking mindfully means having awareness of the articulators and speaking with precision and energy. Here are some tips on how to achieve this:

- To start simply say the days of the week and pay attention to the lips, tongue and jaw shaping the sound. Slow down and notice the movements.
- Now imagine chewing a big piece of chewing gum and moving the whole face, lips and tongue with extra energy. Create a stretch and space – feel the muscles stretch. Good speech is muscular so make sure those muscles are engaged.
- If you can, sing along to some music and really go for it. Engage all the muscles and really move the mouth.
- When speaking focus on getting the ends of the words clear, particularly the end consonant it gives you real clarity.
- Pay attention to vowels and consonants. Vowels communicate the emotion and consonants the sense.
- Try speaking a sentence and overdoing the vowels then the consonants. Then say it again and feel how muscular your speech feels. You can 'bite the words' as the Chinese say.

- Find the balance. Using your speech fully but not overdoing it is the art. Practise and record your voice to get it right.

Principle 4: Speak So Others Listen Toolkit

The beginnings of things arise from natural talent,
and the ends are reached by discipline.
RHETORICA AD HERENNIUM

Practice

Find a daily practice and enjoy doing a little each day, even if it's singing in the shower or reading your children a bedtime story. If it's hard to get started tell yourself you'll only do it for five minutes. Then you'll find you get into it anyway. Make it fun and absorb yourself in it as much as possible. Reward yourself afterwards – it boosts your motivation.

Tone

Don't be a talking head; speak from your heart and gut. Singing is a good way to get the support muscles to kick in or tap the diaphragm – speak/sing when you wake up in the morning (see page 90). In formal moments always project your voice to the back of the room as the intention to send it to the back connects you to the right muscles.

Pause

Speak in neat phrases. Give them each the space they need. Leonard Bernstein said music is what happens between the notes. Communication happens in between your words. You need to give them space to land in the minds of your listeners and you need space to think.

Speak one thought at a time to allow your audience to take in what you have said.

Pace

Get the pace just right for the audience – not too fast, not too slow. Use weight to help you find the right pace. Emphasise the words that matter (the meaning words) so that you make what you say easy to listen to, owned and energised.

Speak Clearly

Articulate words fully and with energy. It allows you to speak at an energised, easy-to-understand pace. Because you shape each word fully you have to take time to connect to what it means, which makes you energised, well paced and easy to listen to.

Be Conversational

Even when you are nervous aim to keep a calm, conversational pace. Imagine talking to one person and giving them time to take in what you have said before you move on to the next idea.

Principle 5: Win Hearts and Minds

How to Inspire, Engage and Influence Your Audience

If your actions inspire others to dream more, learn more,
do more and become more, then you are a leader.
JOHN QUINCY ADAMS, US PRESIDENT

The economist Alfred Marshall used to tell his colleagues to 'Increase the number of those in the world with cool heads and warm hearts.' A warm heart matters as much to gravitas as a cool head and this is the focus of this chapter. Emotion channelled out into the world via your eyes, your voice and your energy is the spark that sets your idea alight and allows it to spread.

Whether you call it pathos (as the Greeks did) or emotional intelligence (as we do these days) be sure of one thing – emotion matters when it comes to gravitas. Aristotle thought emotion was so important that he devoted a whole chapter to it in *The Art Of Rhetoric*. Cicero waxed lyrical, saying that emotion should flow through your speech like blood through the body. He understood that emotion is what moves an audience to really enjoy your words. When you have a connection to your content, the why as much as the what will engage us.[1]

We're going to investigate this driver at the heart of gravitas – the passion that fires you with enthusiasm and makes you compelling to others. I'm going to show you why emotion is essential to balance your logic and give you some tools to help you access yours.

Light the Spark

An idea is powerless if it stays inside of you ...
if you communicate an idea in a way that resonates,
change will happen and you can change the world.

NANCY DUARTE, CEO AND AUTHOR

If you're wondering why emotion matters, you can blame your brain. Descartes should have said, 'I feel, I think, therefore I am.' Think about the last time you made a decision. First you got the gut feeling, good or bad: 'I love that', 'I hate that', 'I'm worried', 'I'm curious'. Then your brain has a little chat with itself and works out the logic to back up the feeling.

What you're experiencing is the activity of two parts of your brain: the neocortex, which does analysis, language, reason and hears the argument; and the limbic system, the seat of emotion, of feeling. And the feeling part tends to win.

The process goes something like this. Your attention is attracted by something new. The information goes to the limbic system, which decides if it is agreeable (true) or disagreeable (false). The limbic system then gives positive emotions to agreeable information or negative emotions to disagreeable information. We form our beliefs and our sense of true and false in this emotional centre. Then we justify our belief in the neocortex; the seat of logic.

When it comes to gravitas the transference of enthusiasm matters as much as the clarity of your reason. When you find the balance between head and heart, reason and emotion (or logos and pathos as Aristotle called it), your gravitas really kicks in.

The Expert Problem

She runs the gamut of emotions from A–B.

DOROTHY PARKER ON KATHARINE HEPBURN

'Help, I've been invited to speak at TED.' (TED stands for Technology, Entertainment and Design and is a global set of conferences addressing a wide range of topics within science and culture.)

My client is a brilliant economist whose career has seen him work both in universities and in finance. It should have been so simple to stand up and dazzle on the TED stage. In theory he'd taught enough to know how to craft and deliver a great talk. He'd also spent a month working hard with a professional speech-writer to get the words just so.

So far, so good. But with a week to go they hit a problem. The speech captured his wisdom but he wasn't making it sing in rehearsal. He sounded flat, a little monotonous – a talking head. He had the classic expert's problem. Too much expertise and not enough emotion.

Everything in moderation is a maxim that applies to analysis. Here the balance you must find for gravitas is between emotion and analysis. Both are essential if you are to influence your audience with your ideas. As much as it matters to get your logos, your reasoning, clear, you can go too far with it. Too much precision makes you seem cold and overly controlled. As philosopher Bertrand Russell put it, 'The degree of one's emotions varies inversely with one's knowledge of the facts.' Sometimes, the more you know the harder it is to get excited about it (and to excite others). When you know too much you get caught up in analysis.

Science is discovering that Bertrand Russell was right. Scientists in Australia put 45 college students under an MRI scanner and presented them with one set of exercises that required them to think about how others might feel and another set of exercises where they had to solve physics problems. What they found is that when the brain fires up empathy, it suppresses the neural network for analysis. And when the networks in the brain fire up for analysis, the neural networks for empathy are repressed. MRI scanners showed that the feeling exercises switched off the parts of the brain used for analysis and switched on its social network. The physics exercises switched off the empathy part of the brain and switched on the analytical network.[2] As Anthony Jack, assistant professor of cognitive science at Case Western Reserve University explains it, the challenge is this:

> You want the CEO of a company to be highly analytical in order to run a company efficiently ... But, you can lose your moral compass if you get stuck in an analytical way of thinking. You never get by without both networks. You don't want to favour one, but cycle efficiently between them and employ the right one at the right time.

The Australian research showed that how we spend our time changes our brains. We need to be aware of the possible blind spots this may cause us to have. Has your training made you more analytical or more emotional? What do you need to do to find the balance?

The difference between analysis and feeling can be symbolised as the difference between head and heart. Both are essential to gravitas. You need to be aware of when you're more removed, and when you're in the moment. You need to be able to change gear between the two.

The Facts Don't Speak for Themselves

One who forms a judgement on any point,
but cannot explain himself to the people, might as
well never have thought at all on the subject.

THUCYDIDES, HISTORIAN

There are some big dangers when clever people don't deliver their ideas with the emotional power that persuades others to listen. After the *Columbia* space shuttle disaster, in which the craft burnt up on re-entry to the earth's atmosphere on 1 February 2003 causing the tragic deaths of its crew, blame was focused on a single piece of foam that separated from the wing as the shuttle took off.

In the investigation that followed scientists made a key discovery. The data had predicted the fault and the warning had been presented before the disaster in a PowerPoint presentation. That the data was there for all to see but wasn't heeded tells us that actually the facts didn't speak for themselves. The data was clear to the logical mind but without powerful delivery, the appeal to the emotions, the warning went unheard, with tragic consequences for the astronauts and their families.

Don't make the same mistake. People only listen if you grab their attention. Data doesn't grab their attention, *you* have to do that. You have to set them alight with the spark of your energy.

Flex feeling and Thinking

Wherever you start from, analysis or feeling, the art to gravitas is to flex between the two.

Analytical people, with the ideas that come from years and years of study, need to be able to take themselves into feeling and passion to express themselves to others. Think of the passion of Nobel Prize-winning physicist Richard Feynman, who was involved in the inquiry that followed the *Challenger* disaster. Look up his lectures on YouTube – his sheer energy, wit and chutzpah bring his subject to vivid life.

Feeling people need to be able to step back and see the big picture, to analyse and consider. Think of the balance of feeling and analysis in good broadcasters – connection and thoughtfulness is a powerful combination.

Whatever You Feel, They Feel

> *The emotions aren't always immediately subject to reason,*
> *but they are almost immediately subject to action.*
>
> WILLIAM JAMES, PHILOSOPHER AND PSYCHOLOGIST

My TED client (see page 107, subsequently referred to as Mr TED) had made a career out of his analytical brain but this next step up in his career required boldness. He needed power, enthusiasm and energy. He needed passion. What had got him here – thought, hard work, intellect, wouldn't get him there – the enthusiasm that would fire up his audience and earn him a standing ovation. This enthusiasm is what gives you 'muchness' as the Mad Hatter puts it, the glow of energy and emotion.

The Roman poet and satirist Horace said, 'Whatever I feel they feel.' Modern science backs this up. Emotions are contagious. If a speaker is engaged and enthusiastic about their content an audience picks up that excitement. If the speaker is analytical and disconnected then that is what the audience will feel about the content.

We had to find a way to get Mr TED out of his head and into his emotion. Fortunately there's a quick way to do this if you know how. In neurolinguistic programming (NLP) there is a useful distinction made between being in feeling – *associated* emotionally, where you're in the experience looking out through your own eyes, and being *disassociated* and analytical – where you are seeing the whole thing from a distance.

Both are important. Being able to associate and disassociate yourself at will is key to gravitas because you can step into passion, energy and charisma and then step back into objectivity at will. For example, athletes need to stay associated in the body to feel the fine-tuning of the muscles and their movement. But when things go wrong it's important for them to be able to disassociate from coaching criticism so they can learn from it objectively and move on.

Mr TED delivered his speech brilliantly on the day, having put the required work in. He found the right balance between his incisive analysis and his passion and power as a speaker. It took courage. Mr TED was naturally very good at stepping back from the data and analysing it. There were many moments in his talk where it was useful for him to allow the audience to do the same. To make a conscious decision to step back and think, and to be aware of the effect it would have on his audience.

Because his data was exact it worked out in a logical step-by-step process that gave him certainty. He was cool with that. The scary part was the emotion. He was terrified as he paced around the green room before his talk. Connecting to his feelings felt risky, more of an art, a chemical reaction between him, his ideas and the room. The alchemy could only happen in the moment and he had to trust that and drop into the fear. Only by letting go a little could he take the audience with him. As he stepped out on stage he dived in. He breathed, smiled at the audience and took the speech moment by moment, owning every word, feeling every emotion. It worked. He got a standing ovation. As he walked off stage a great big grin extended across his face from ear to ear.

As Mr TED discovered, association and disassociation are both key to gravitas. Let's work out your current style and then let's think about how to adjust it to get the maximum impact when you speak. It's about when to use heart, when to use mind and how to flex between the two so you get the results you want.

Try This 1: Head or Heart Questionnaire

Are you more of an analytical, disassociated person or a feeling, associated person when the going gets tough? We all do both but tend to get stuck in one or the other in challenging moments.

Let's map the two states first so you know the difference, then I'll show you how to move between them. Below is a grid to help you decide if you are more in your head or your heart. Choose which description fits you best professionally (and check in to see if you do something different in your personal life).

	A – Heart *Presence: you are mostly connected – in the experience.*	B – Head *Distance: you are mostly outside something – observing, detached.*
Perspective	• In your own body, present and tuned in to your feelings and those of other people. • You see things looking out from your own eyes.	• You are stepped back – seeing things from a distance. See things 'over there'. • You sometimes see your body from the outside, as if on a movie screen. • You are more in your thoughts than emotions, reflective, analytical.
Awareness of time	• You are mostly in the moment. You often lose track of time, becoming completely absorbed.	• You spend most of your time thinking about past and future, analysing, assessing, planning.
Voice	• Lots of range and rich resonance. Engaging and inspiring.	• Flatter tone, thoughtful and considered voice. Analytical.
Body	• Tuned in to feeling in body and emotional state • Lean forward, bright eyes, colour in cheeks. Passionate.	• Disconnected from feelings – in analysis. • Lean back and focus eyes away, sense that you are distant. Reflective, cool-headed.

Count up how many of your answers are from column A and how many from column B.

Mostly A answers You are more associated in life – more heart/emotional. Your challenge is to find more structure and you'll benefit from developing your analysis. Take time to step back and reflect sometimes. See the world from a distance, especially when you get overwhelmed. Take the feeling out of it by getting some perspective. You can even imagine standing on top of a big hill looking down on the scene from far away. It's about being able to choose to make decisions without being overwhelmed by emotion. See Mind: Find Your Objectivity (How to Disassociate), overleaf.

Mostly B answers You are more disassociated – more head/analytical. You need the same programme as Mr TED, to engage emotionally. The trick is to get into your emotions, into your values, so you can really connect and have conviction and enthusiasm. That way you'll inspire your audience too. See Heart: Find Your Enthusiasm (How to Associate), overleaf.

Mix of A and B answers You are well balanced between emotion and analysis, which is a good basis for gravitas. Your challenge now is to up your game – to develop both your association and your disassociation so you can do both when needed.

Try This 2: Heart and Head –
How to Use Association and Disassociation

There are two ways to live your life. One is as though
nothing is a miracle. The other is as though everything is.
ALBERT EINSTEIN, THEORETICAL PHYSICIST

Heart: Find Your Enthusiasm (How to Associate)

If you want to enjoy the moment and really be present (and have presence and charisma) step into *association*. The good moments in life are best enjoyed in association – in the here and now, not 'over there'. Plus being in your body, fully alive and engaged is the best way to fire up an audience. If you want to be more associated in life your beliefs are a good place to start. What you believe about life tunes you into the heart of the gravitas equation – your knowledge, your purpose, your passion. Go back to Principle 3, I Believe (see page 68). If you can write down five beliefs that really fire you up you are well on the road to association – and to igniting the interest of your audience.

Mind: Find Your Objectivity (How to Disassociate)

Analysis and objectivity require *disassociation*. Bad memories and feelings are easier when you get some distance and detach from them. If the situation is uncomfortable or there are negative emotions it can be really helpful to step back and view it with some objectivity.[3]

Flex

The table opposite contains tips to help you flex between a warm heart – the passion and engaging energy of association, with the cool head and analysis of disassociation, where you step back and see the bigger picture.

To Associate	To Disassociate
Get into your body. Do a physical warm-up, whether it's running first thing or walking or some light stretches. Anything that gently gets you into your body is good.	Step back from the situation in your mind's eye. Imagine looking down on it from a long way away. Get distance from it to take the emotion out.
Be fully in your senses. See what you see, hear what you hear, feel what you feel, out there in the world.	If negative emotions crowd in, imagine the scene is on a smartphone screen and that you can push it away into the distance until it is tiny.
Tell personal stories to connect you. Bring the data to life.	If someone's voice is making you feel bad, imagine turning the volume down until you can't hear them anymore or imagine they sound like Mickey Mouse.

Take the Audience on a Journey

The most profound joy has more of gravity than of gaiety in it.
MICHEL DE MONTAIGNE, WRITER

The word emotion comes from the Latin *movere*, to move. If you can take your audience on a journey with you in the service of a purpose greater than you then you are on the path to powerful communication. It's the change in emotions that grips us. It's a roller coaster we want to hang on tight to, waiting to see what happens next.

The lessons are in movies, in theatre, in the dramatic arc (see overleaf). Think of the emotional arc of a movie or a play. A good director takes you through a roller coaster of feelings. You go through pain and pleasure, fear and excitement and at the end of a good film you feel changed by it. Good speakers understand that they must affect their audience like this. If your audience is not changed by what you have said then you have not made impact.

Beware. Using this kind of emotion to pitch something purely in your own interest may be compelling but it lacks the compassion and generosity of heart that makes it gravitas – the difference between Simon Cowell and Barack Obama. Both are skilled at emotion, but are very different in their respective levels of gravitas. Charisma works brilliantly when employed for selfish purposes, gravitas less so. Gravitas needs heart and soul to make it work.

The Dramatic Arc

> *What comes from the heart goes to the heart.*
> SAMUEL TAYLOR COLERIDGE, POET, CRITIC AND PHILOSOPHER

As we've discovered, emotion is all about movement. This applies to engaging your audience – if you want to move an audience you need to ensure your emotions move first. What you feel, they feel. When you think like a movie director and take your audience on an emotional journey, you engage them.

What you'll need is what Aristotle outlined as the structure of great tragedy, and later German novelist and playwright Gustav Freytag described as the 'dramatic arc'.[4] You will find the dramatic arc everywhere when you start to look for it – in films, plays, novels, even in adverts.

It works like this:

- Inciting event
- Conflict
- Rising tension
- Denouement
- Falling action

How to Use Your Emotion to Be a Compelling Speaker

So how do you change your gear emotionally? Cicero, a believer in moving an audience via the emotions, said that the two basic gears were *gentleness* and *vehemence*. Neuro-economics pioneer Paul Zak has found that research results back up Cicero's belief in these emotional gear changes. The emotions that matter, Zak says, are stress and connection. Zak discovered that applying the dramatic arc has startling effects resulting in measurable hormonal changes in audiences. And measurable engagement too.

Zak told volunteers at his lab the story of a little boy called Ben. Ben is suffering from cancer but is a happy little boy because he has finished his treatment and he loves playing with his father. But his father feels sadness because even as he watches Ben's happiness, he knows Ben is dying.

In Zak's story the *inciting event* is a sad one. The little boy has cancer. This sets up a *conflict* in the father, of knowing that his beautiful boy is dying and yet his son is happy to play and live in the moment. This creates the *rising tension* of the coming climax. How can Ben's father engage playfully knowing his son is dying? One of the key features of the dramatic arc is that you start with the end in mind. You know where the story is leading – to the *denouement* where Ben's father finds a way to play with his son and enjoy the moment and *falling action* (the end of the story, the wrap-up) where Ben's father reflects. The father says straight to the camera, 'You don't know what it feels like to know how little time you have left.'

Though it is hard not to be moved by the story, Zak's research shows that the emotions it causes via the structure of the dramatic arc can be used to trigger positive action. Moderate distress makes us engage. It makes us act. Researchers discovered (when they took blood from volunteers before and after the story) that when listeners felt distress at the beginning of the story their system produced cortisol – a hormone that focuses attention on something important. Then at the end, when Ben's father reflects on the power of knowing how little time one has left, volunteers felt empathy and produced oxytocin – the hormone of care and connection. When it came to the end of the experiment those who had experienced these emotions were far more likely to donate money to a children's charity.

As Zak says, 'Through oxytocin release, these products of the human imagination connect us to the entire human family. This is what we want as social creatures.' Stories change minds. If you choose stories that have meaning for you and connect to the common purpose you fire up the gravitas equation, and with it your innate gravitas. You also stand a very good chance of moving your listeners to take action.[5]

Try This: Journey of Analysis and Emotion

Every time you present, you're given an opportunity to plan a journey, tune into the audience's resonant frequency, and move them to action.

NANCY DUARTE, CEO AND AUTHOR

People will remember what you make them feel. When you prepare content for an audience remember that you must balance analysis with emotion.

- Making conscious choices is key. Be intentional about the energy you bring to each section. You have the power to change the mood of the audience. Where do you plan to take them?
- On your script mark the emotion you want the audience to feel at each point. Whether you draw a big smiley face or write 'excitement', 'wonder', 'thoughtful', etc. at different points in the script

is entirely up to you. You might introduce an emotion at the beginning and then come back to it at the end.

- The greatest test of whether it's working? Notice the responses of your audience. Are they engaged and awake or nodding off? If you're aware of how people are responding you will always know what emotion they need next.

Principle 5: Win Hearts and Minds Toolkit

You've lost your muchness ... You used to be much ... muchier.
MAD HATTER, *ALICE IN WONDERLAND*

Man cannot live by data alone. You need to give your speech the spark of emotion to persuade and inspire an audience. Here's how.

Find the Why

If you want to fire up your passion remember why you're doing this speech. Some good questions are:

- What's exciting about this idea/project for you?
- What has surprised you about it?
- What has made you laugh? Laughter is the most direct route between two brains; find the humour.
- What has frustrated you? Frustration and anger are often the richest sources of comedy and stories.
- What do you particularly love about it? What stories can you tell? Keep it specific: people, places, sights, sounds, feelings.
- What's the dream? What will success look like when you achieve it? (Think Martin Luther King.) Paint the vision in simple words or in powerful images.

- What's in it for your audience? Write down a list of benefits from their perspective and in their language.

Tell Stories

Stories, says researcher and writer Brene Brown, are 'data with a soul'.[6] And stories, especially your own, are the quickest shortcut to emotion. Above all when shaping a story it helps to remember to start with the end in mind. What's the purpose of the story? Then learn the key bullet points and practise telling the story in a relaxed conversational way.

Step into the Emotion

Use emotional memory. The act of bringing to mind a happy memory in your life allows you to access that same emotion now. It works for any emotion you want the audience to feel. First, feel it yourself, then let it be expressed through your voice and body language. If you feel it, so do the audience. The more you can be in the experience – associated into it – the more compelling it will be for the audience. Refine this as you rehearse and practise stepping into the story. You don't need to show us you're feeling it, you just need to feel and we'll get it. Then you have gears should you need them to adjust your energy to take the audience where they need to go. If they look like they need a boost, up your energy. If they need a moment to think, make your tone more reflective. See your voice and energy as a way of changing the energy of the audience. Treat what you say almost like a piece of music, find the emotional rise and fall.

Principle 6: Keep an Open Mind and a Level Head

How to be Understanding and Influential Around Tricky People

*The significant problems that we face cannot be solved
at the same level of thinking with which we created them.*
ALBERT EINSTEIN, THEORETICAL PHYSICIST

The ability to keep an open mind and a level head is the sixth principle of gravitas. It's the big one when it comes to your influence and wisdom. The mind is like a parachute. It works best when opened. And the best way to open your mind and stay on the right side of the law? You'll need what psychologists call cognitive flexibility. This is the ability to take perspectives very different to your own and to suspend judgement and see a different side to the issue before you make the decision. This mind-stretching can all happen very quickly once you learn how it works and it will work wonders for the empathy and influence so key to gravitas.

The Greeks saw this cognitive (and physical) flexibility as so important that they had a goddess of shape-shifting called Metis. She was often represented as an octopus because of her ability to help wrestlers and orators wriggle out of difficulties. Metis was very much in demand. Zeus, the king of the gods, wanted her wisdom so much that he swallowed her.

If you'd like to know a little more about finding your own Metis, your own flexibility, it helps to start with the golden rule of gravitas.

The Golden Rule

Everything we hear is an opinion, not a fact.
Everything we see is a perspective, not the truth.
MARCUS AURELIUS, ROMAN EMPEROR AND PHILOSOPHER

Two theatre producers are sitting in a London theatre green room discussing a new season of productions when in rushes the director of the show that opens that week, anxiety etched across his face. He starts to shout about the disaster that has befallen the technical rehearsal in the theatre: '*You* have created this mess. You are responsible for a flawed show – you need to come and talk to the cast.'

The senior producer looks at him. 'Michael,' she says, 'please remember the golden rule.' Michael pauses; thinks. He asks if the senior producer can attend the notes session after the rehearsal. She says she will. After a thoughtful moment calm is restored and he makes his exit, apologising, with a wry grin.

As the producers work out the structure of their new season, the door to the green room is roughly pushed open again. In storms Eddie the production designer, in full voice. 'It's all my fault, I have ruined everything, you must hate me.' He gesticulates wildly about the argument escalating outside the room. 'Eddie,' says the senior producer, 'the golden rule please.' Silence. After a moment of contemplation, and a request to meet later that day, the designer exits, looking calmer.

As the producers get back to their planning there's an angry knock at the door. In comes the stage manager, fuming and complaining loudly, 'They can't even obey the basic rules. Having analysed the various problems I cannot see how we can proceed.'

'Elise,' says the senior producer, 'please remember the golden rule.' Elise gives a tired smile and suggests they discuss it in the team meeting that afternoon and leaves.

The junior producer looks at her boss with wonder. 'Please, tell me what the golden rule is.'

'Ah,' says the senior producer. 'Don't take everything so damn personally – and lighten up.'[1]

Make the golden rule your gravitas mantra. *More problems in life are caused because we take offence than by others giving offence.*

See bad behaviour as turbulence and keep your pilot of the plane cool; don't take it personally. Negative emotion is contagious. It makes everyone grumpy – fast. If you notice the bad behaviour and deal with it you can stop the contagion. This Metis, or resourcefulness, gives you grace under fire, and as such it's massively gravitas-boosting.

Meet the Gremlins

Whenever you are about to find fault with someone,
ask yourself the following question: 'What fault of mine
most nearly resembles the one I am about to criticise?'
MARCUS AURELIUS, ROMAN EMPEROR AND PHILOSOPHER

To deal with tricky people it's useful to be able to recognise four key patterns of bad behaviour. We're going to call them the *gremlins*. You've already met three of them in The Golden Rule (see opposite): Michael hides his fear by blaming others; Eddie becomes a distracting whirlwind of stress; and Elise deals with fear by disconnecting from emotion. These are three of the four gremlins: *blamer, distractor* and *computer*. The gremlin we haven't met yet is *placator*.

The gremlins are the bad-boy behaviours that will put your gravitas and pilot-of-the-plane-ness to the test. Big time.

Dealing with bad behaviour is about being able to step back and see the patterns rather than getting sucked into the toxic soup of blame and counter-blame. If you can avoid that two-fingered salute and start to see that most difficult relationships have a pattern – a cast list of roles in which everyone takes on their own role, gets a little typecast and usually plays up to it – then you can make changes.

These four patterns come from the work of family therapist Virginia Satir who identified four universal patterns of fear-driven communication.[2] They are the stressed out versions of the archetypes we met in Principle 2.

1. **Blame** – to put the fault on the other person (stressed out warrior).
2. **Placate** – to appease the other person to avoid anger (stressed out carer).
3. **Compute** – to hide behind words and to ignore any threats, hoping they'll go away (stressed out king/queen).
4. **Distract** – to hide by changing the subject (stressed out creator).

Satir spent many years working with clients and observing the different forces in dysfunctional family relationships in her family-therapy practice. She kept seeing four very specific patterns (note that Satir didn't refer to the patterns as gremlins, that's my term for them) showing up in toxic relationships and she realised that there was a way to detox these negative patterns.

Satir worked out that when someone is feeling 'low-pot' – an expression based on an old cooking pot that was kept in the centre of the stove at her family home – their self-esteem has cooked away under all the pressures of life and work. When that happens they feel unhappy, self-critical and unsafe. Essentially low-pot is when negative emotions overwhelm us – when we lose control, lose our temper and feel anxious.

Satir's observation was that when you're feeling low-pot, four disruptive behaviours tend to come galloping grumpily into the room. These disruptive behaviours are used to mask what's going on inside – all the feelings of fear and anxiety. They are the opposite of gravitas, which is about the ability to make the inner and the outer self-synchronised and congruent. But the more you know about these incongruent behaviours the better you are able to deal with them when they show up. Chances are you'll recognise them instantly. We've all worked with most of these four gremlins in our time and they can be a huge obstacle to gravitas and influence. They are simple to neutralise when you understand that fear and anxiety drive them.

1. Blamer

The *blamer* gremlin feels fear and points the finger to hide it. Blame destroys relationships because it triggers anxiety and judgement and kills listening and understanding. Pointing and shouting may seem powerful but it's a hollow kind of power.

Want to know what the blamer is like? Go and stand in front of the mirror, stare and then point your finger aggressively. Try saying the days of the week. Go on, spit them out, one after the other.

Nasty isn't it? The blamer is the stereotypical sergeant major, the school bully. Lacking the control of the warrior, their energy becomes aggressive.

Blamers:

- Are fault-finders
- Think they are right
- Want others to obey them.

Why? They are frightened, that's why. And the more frightened they are the more they blame others. Picture a little kitten fluffing itself up in the face of a big old cat. They try to make themselves look bigger, stronger.

In their little heads is a big, booming voice that's telling them they must stay in control, that they must be dominant. That's because they're frightened and they're petrified of someone finding them out. So they try to hide their terror.

Blamers often start their sentences with: 'You never', 'Why do you always' and 'Why can't you'. You'll hear them use the word 'you' a lot when they are criticising. *You! You!*

Much of the time blamers don't let people finish their sentences. They interrupt, they don't listen and above all they don't take responsibility. Everyone else is the problem. It's never the blamer's fault.

To make matters worse, blamers don't take people with them or convince them to take their point of view. They just frighten people into submission.

Blamers don't learn or evolve. They get stuck. As Virginia Satir says, we 'lose our ability to steer the situation in another direction, to learn from it.' And, of course, the blamer loses their gravitas because they are not in control. They react to fear and anxiety in a knee-jerk way.

Blamer at its worst is all anxiety with little self-awareness, it's largely a gravitas-free zone. However, if you can step into blamer for strategic purposes without feeling fear or anxiety and without losing your temper then it can work in very small doses. This is the adult equivalent of the naughty step. But as soon as fear or anxiety drives it or as soon as you lose control it's game over as far as your gravitas is concerned.

In order for blamers to become people who create harmony rather than stress in life (and to find the empathy and influence key to gravitas) blamers need to:

- Disagree without blaming
- Control fear and anxiety and to take responsibility for it
- Turn it into warrior power (see page 50) to move things forward
- Give their view, see the wider context and express what they need.

2. Placator

The *placator* gremlin fears being rejected, disliked and disagreed with, so they are desperate to say the right thing.

To get yourself into the head of the placator put your palms up in front of you defensively, raise your eyebrows and then open your arms wide. Move your head a lot and make yourself the victim. Your shoulders will sag, your arms will feel weak and psychologically you'll feel weaker too.

Placators:

- Are afraid of disagreeing
- Rarely stand up for themselves
- Don't push their own views forward
- Apologise for things that aren't their fault.

Placators can be seen as yes-men. They show classic passive-aggressive people-pleasing energy. They tend to say yes to everything irrespective of what they actually think and that makes others feel guilty. That nice person who appears to agree with everyone can be highly damaging to projects. Placators are silent, smiling saboteurs – often because they're too scared to tell you they disagree. They may say yes to your face but when they leave the room they know full well that they won't do anything different. Nothing changes, even after months of meetings, when you have placators in the room.

They want to be everyone's friend, everyone's favourite colleague. They say things like, 'Whatever you think', 'I want to make you happy' and 'I'll go with everyone else's decision.' Placators want to put others first. Their level of self-worth is so low that they think they're unimportant and that their needs and ideas aren't worth considering. In their minds everyone is superior to them. You have no idea what they really think and for that reason they have no ethos, no definition and no gravitas. People-pleaser placators lack backbone. They sound and look like pushovers.

In order to find the courage to speak their own minds (key to the authority of gravitas) placators need to:

- Know what they want for themselves and balance it with the needs of others – meeting your own needs even as you help others is key to sustainable, healthy relationships
- Understand that they can't please all the people all the time
- Know that it's okay to speak their truth and stand firm as long as they are open to others' views too
- Learn to apologise for an act not their existence
- Channel their care for others into carer (see page 50).

3. Computer

The *computer* is the uber-correct, super-reasonable type who lives in the world of the mind. This gremlin loses their gravitas because fear makes them cut off from their emotions and live in their reason. In the gravitas equation they may have knowledge but they lack the passion that communicates it.

To get into computer mode keep your body very still as if your spine is a steel rod. Put your hand on your chin and speak. Notice that this takes your eyes down and your focus inwards. Say the days of the week and listen to what happens to your vocal tone. It's flat, dry, dull, devoid of emotion and often nasal in tone.

Computers are vulnerable. They may believe they are above all that emotion and self-esteem stuff, but they are scared of showing their real selves. When they feel like this they hide behind what they often perceive is superior knowledge and an insistence on being correct in all areas and on all subjects. They cover up their feelings of social inadequacy by being punctilious and accurate at all times. For them, making a mistake is the ultimate nightmare.

Computers:

- Approach everything with ice-cold logic
- Use their extensive vocabulary or knowledge to belittle others
- Often fail to understand the feelings of others
- Insist on strict adherence to process and practice.

The computer gremlin uses big words as a smokescreen but this ultra-reasonable language sucks the life out of their interactions. When vulnerability hits they shut it down with logic and distance themselves with scientific language. They keep themselves busy being correct and choosing the right words. For them accuracy is king.

In order to communicate in a way that is authentic and interesting to others (key to the passion required for gravitas – see Principle 5) computers need to:

- Learn that they can be reasonable with emotion
- Reason without being dry and boring
- Feel safe to express emotion.

4. Distractor

Distractors feel the fear and get into a wild spin. They change the subject at dizzying speed and change their minds even faster. They are human whirlwinds, at the centre of which is a deep fear that if they stop moving someone will find them out.

To slip into the role of distractor think Italian-style gestures, over-the-top movements, arms waving wildly and expressively. Talk in a sing-song voice, varying the pitch. Then change the subject. Jump from one topic to another. You might notice a very unfocused kind of energy, like a spinning top.

Distractors:

- Are unfocused and don't keep to the point
- Are bouncy and uncontrolled, like a human Tigger
- Tend to talk quickly
- Gloss over important points and veer off at tangents
- Change subjects, rarely stopping for breath.

The distractor likes the smokescreen they create. They want people to be fuddled and confused and lose track of what they're trying to say. It covers up their uncertainty. Distractors dramatise to prevent others from noticing the unease underneath.

The distractor tries to be so wildly visible that they effectively become invisible to everyone. By using dizzying and ungrounded behaviour the distractor can upset meetings and leave them in complete disarray with nothing resolved. They are frequently exhausting to deal with.

In order to find the focus and honesty to say what they think rather than hiding behind a smokescreen of distraction, distractors need to:

- Learn to connect to their purpose and find resolution
- Know that it's safe to talk without distracting others
- Change the subject without being distracting
- Feel comfortable in who they are.

Leveller

Levellers distinguish between what they are feeling and the
thoughts they express with words. They take into account their
and others feelings, thoughts, realities and words.
VIRGINIA SATIR, FAMILY THERAPIST

If you *can* keep your head when faced by blaming, placating, computing or distracting (think of the senior producer in The Golden Rule story, see page 122) then you have gravitas and influence.

But though it's easy to talk about gravitas and influence, when faced by the gremlins and seeing the red mist they tend to provoke they are hard to hold on to.

Luckily Satir worked out a highly effective antidote to the gremlins, a flak jacket for the soul. Satir realised that the only way to 'detox' the gremlins is with what she calls a 'leveller'. Levellers act with gravitas – they have knowledge, purpose and passion and express themselves calmly, honestly and empathetically. They stay calm when dealing with the gremlins. They get relationships back on an even keel and restore peace.

Leveller behaviour can most definitely be learnt and there are two very good reasons why you should. Firstly, it saves your relationships. The marriage therapist John Gottman says that because of the brain's defensive 'negativity bias' it takes five good experiences to make up for one bad red-mist/gremlin one.[3] Secondly, levellers earn more. In one study on a management consultancy the main difference between high-earning and low-earning partners was the ability of the high earners to be levellers (or to self-regulate as psychologists call it). Why? We like being led by people who can lead themselves well, even when trouble hits.

So, how do you learn to be a leveller?

There are three key tools you need and we're going to look at each in turn:

1. **Set yourself free** The five freedoms
2. **Walk a mile in their shoes** Empathy and understanding
3. **Extend yourself** Build trust and connection

Set Yourself Free: The Five Freedoms

The first rule of leveller is to set yourself free from the negative thinking that triggers the gremlins. What tends to trigger gremlins are moments when we feel un-appreciated, left out, misunderstood or that our achievements are not being recognised. The five freedoms help you to set yourself free from the opinions of others when you find yourself in a negative and anxious state of mind. If you get rid of the niggles you often get rid of the gremlins and into a more positive leveller state of mind.[4]

1. **The freedom to see and hear what is here (not what should be)** 'Should', 'ought', 'must'. These are gremlin-triggering words. The sense that Mrs Jones is watching and that things must be a certain way. Even if Mrs Jones is in your head, sod the rules. Levellers accept what *is* rather than what should be. This frees you to enjoy life rather than worrying all the time. If Mrs Jones triggers anxiety you may find that it helps to remember that Mrs Jones has a Mrs Jones and is probably feeling just as anxious as you.

2. **The freedom to say what you feel and think** Levellers are aware and direct. They level with people. The inner and the outer are congruent. You express your feelings and accept your thoughts as valid and voice them. But make sure you know what you are really communicating, don't just judge from inside – check it out. 'Warm

and friendly' in your head is no good when your demeanour shows at best 'screen-saver face' and at worst 'bitchy resting face'. Check in the mirror and record your voice. Face the truth. If in doubt, ask. Tough? Maybe, but at least you will know what other people see and hear and you'll know how to adjust when others react strangely to you. The answer is sometimes as simple as 'lighten up'.

3. **The freedom to feel what you feel** Accept what you feel rather than thinking you should feel something else. (Go back to Try This: Tune into True North on page 35 to help with this.) Allow others to feel what they feel – accept it.

4. **The freedom to ask for what you need** Speak up. If you don't understand, ask. Or as Satir puts it:

> People sometimes seem to feel they will be thought ignorant if they don't understand. When this happens to me I ask people to repeat, and I usually tell them I have not heard clearly and I want to.

If you ask you learn something and you grow. Most people like to be asked if you do it at the right moment. And it's often the case that if you're in company others are also confused. Ask gracefully – explain that you want to understand and others will happily explain. When you use powerful questions (sparingly) they often help everyone deepen their understanding.

5. **The freedom to take risks on your own behalf** Be bold. You don't have to wait for permission. Levellers don't stay swaddled by their comfort zone. They have the boldness to try new things knowing that, as Satir said, it's all good if you allow yourself to be a slow learner and to take the pressure off.

Walk a Mile In Their Shoes: Empathy and Understanding

When another blames you or hates you, or people voice similar criticisms, go to their souls, penetrate inside and see what sort of people they are. You will realize that there is no need to be racked with anxiety that they should hold any particular opinion about you.

MARCUS AURELIUS, ROMAN EMPEROR AND PHILOSOPHER

Cognitive flexibility is yoga for the mind. Empathy and understanding require you to stretch your thinking. These behaviours are highly leveller – and highly gravitas. They give you influence and they give you wisdom. You take time to listen before you judge. You see the world from different points of view.

At Harvard they call this ability to see multiple perspectives, to take on ideas counter to your own, as the 'self-transforming mind'. It's best explained by what Virginia Satir said about relationships: '*We meet naturally on the basis of our sameness and grow on the basis of our differentness.*' The self-transforming mind allows you to grow. Studies show that this trait is rare in leadership but it is crucial to learn it (and make no mistake – it is a learnable trait) if you want gravitas. It allows you to meet challenges/challenging people and learn from them. Robert Kegan, professor of adult learning at Harvard's graduate school says that the self-transforming mind has 'the ability to make space for new ideas within a framework, to accept that ideas and situations evolve.' The self-transforming mind actually allows you to welcome new and challenging information. As Kegan says, those with this habit 'Place a higher priority on information that may also alert them to the limits of their current design or frame … it's useful to be more receptive to new ideas, be more flexible in your responses.'[5]

The word you need is *and* as opposed to *but*. *And* has the power to tame gremlins and boost your gravitas in the face of extreme provocation. The open-minded 'I think this, *and* you think that' as opposed to the closed 'I think this *but* you think that'. You suspend your view of the world, take on their views and consider how they got there. Then you can go back to your perspective with new information and new flexibility. The best way to get from *but* to *and* is to try out their perspective. It's why the Norwegian prime minister recently spent a day working as a taxi driver so that he could learn about the views of his electorate.

Empathy

> *If you wish to persuade me, you must think my thoughts,*
> *feel my feelings and speak my words.*
>
> CICERO, ROMAN STATESMAN, ORATOR AND WRITER

When it comes to the self-transforming mind the essential piece of your leveller toolkit is an understanding of the three kinds of empathy. Effectively there are three gears for understanding what someone else is experiencing:

1. **Cognitive empathy** You try to think the way someone else thinks.
2. **Emotional empathy** You imagine how someone is feeling and try on those feelings for yourself.
3. **Empathic concern** You keep an objective distance to your empathy and give someone what they need.

Levellers can flex between 'I think what you think', 'I feel what you feel' and 'I give you what you need' as the context requires. Sometimes you need all three kinds of empathy, for example when a friend needs your help and actively asks for advice. At other times you will strategically choose just one or two kinds of empathy because you need to stay objective. A leveller doctor requires 'I think what you think' and 'I give you what you need'. 'I feel what you feel' is used more sparingly as it can quickly lead to burnout in a caring profession. Even doctors with a good bedside manner know that emotional empathy needs to be rationed.

Knowing the difference between the three kinds of empathy and using them with awareness is key to boosting your gravitas and keeping the gremlins firmly at bay.

The table below will help you assess what kind/s of empathy are required in the situations you face. It shows you: the type of empathy, the benefit to using it and the downside to using it.

For example, if you're a doctor dealing with 50 seriously ill people a day you'll need to be mostly in columns A and C because feeling what they feel when four of the people you see each day are dying is simply unsustainable and will affect your ability to be a good doctor.

But to return to the example of helping a friend. Say your friend wants to tell you about a break-up and simply needs a shoulder to cry on and an ear, then columns A and B are perfect. And if they ask for your advice you can step into column C. Be wary of too much of C – most people have the answers they need. If you can listen in A and B and ask enough questions people usually find the solutions themselves. Gravitas is often about giving someone the space to do that. And then, when asked for advice, being comfortable to step resolutely and clearly into C, 'Here's what I think you should do'.

	A *Cognitive Empathy* *'I think what you think'*	B *Emotional Empathy* *'I feel what you feel'*	C *Empathic Concern* *'I give what you need'*
Benefit	'I understand how you think about things. I can see things from your perspective without feeling what you feel.'	'I feel with you.' Emotional synchrony is great for building harmony and rapport.	'I see you're in trouble and want to help you out.'

	A *Cognitive Empathy* *'I think what you think'*	B *Emotional Empathy* *'I feel what you feel'*	C *Empathic Concern* *'I give what you need'*
Downside	Without emotional empathy this can seem a little manipulative.	Picking up on the distress of others can lead to burnout and exhaustion, especially when you are tuning into distressing emotions. As a result, it needs to be used with awareness if you are in a caring profession.	Don't jump in too quickly with 'I know, …' telling the person what to do. Help them find the solution they need.
How to Do it	Ask yourself 'How is this person thinking in this situation? What are they seeing and feeling?' See both sides of an argument. Accept their view as valid. Listen for keywords and values. Use those words yourself. Ask questions with those words.	Imagine how you would feel in their shoes. You can practise when you read. Imagine how it would feel if it were happening to you.	Depersonalise – see this as part of a bigger context. Think about what has caused this problem to happen. What's the bigger picture – the cause and effect? Ask how you can help. How can you work together? Take action that improves the situation. Identify problems and work to solve them.

Try This: Understanding – Put Yourself in Their Shoes

We have three relationships: one to this bodily shell which envelops us, one to the Divine Cause which is the source of everything in all things; and our fellow mortals around us.

MARCUS AURELIUS, ROMAN EMPEROR AND PHILOSOPHER

Once you've got the theory of empathy the next step is to apply it to your own life, to step into the shoes of someone you find difficult. To think what they think and to feel what they feel so that you can go a little way to giving them what they need.

When you take time to walk a mile in a tricky person's shoes a funny thing happens. You often start to understand them a little more. You start to see the truth in Virginia Satir's maxim, 'People are doing the best they can.' If you can see yourself as they see you and move out of judgement into a space of curiosity about them, and you, and the dynamic between you. Then you start to develop the flexibility of mind so key to gravitas and to influence.

This exercise takes you into three perspectives: yours, theirs (the shoes of a person you find tricky) and a coach position to give yourself advice from. In each perspective you flex your thinking, your feeling and even your movement. You see the world as you see it, then you see the world as they see it, feel what they feel, think what they think. Then you step back to see the dynamic between you and you become your own wise coach with the insight and perspective that comes by stepping back and flexing your thinking. It's a leveller habit – and one that massively boosts your gravitas. It gives you deep wisdom that comes of continually learning from those you meet. You learn little when you judge, loads when you listen.

(If you prefer to listen to this exercise being explained you'll find it on www.gravitasmethod.com.)

You need:

- An empty room
- Three chairs
- An open mind

Using three chairs allows you to see the situation from a different perspective, literally and metaphorically. Once you've done the exercise physically moving from chair to chair a few times you'll find that you can progress and instead of moving physically make the moves only cognitively.

1. You

Your perspective on the situation. What are you thinking, feeling and what do you need? Name what's important to you. What will success look like? What's the fear? How do you perceive the other person?

2. Them

> *When I wish to find out how wise or stupid or how good or*
> *how wicked is anyone, or what are his thoughts at the moment;*
> *I fashion the expression of my face, as accurately as possible,*
> *in accordance with the expression of his, and then wait to see*
> *what thoughts or sentiments arise in my mind or heart,*
> *as if to match or correspond with his expression.*
> EDGAR ALLAN POE, WRITER, POET AND CRITIC

Here, take on their perspective on the situation: what are they thinking, feeling and what do they need?

As Poe suggests above (and as actors know all too well), if you can it really helps to sit like they sit, adopt their facial expression and use their language. It opens up a new part of you, with accompanying new insights.

What will success look like? What's the fear? Notice the values they hold dear and their focus. Try it on for size. Walk a mile in their shoes.

3. Coach

In this position you step back, look at the two chairs and suspend your own perspective and that of the other person. You focus on the dynamic of the relationship, 'the space between' as actors call it. You see the different perspectives on the situation and hold both of them at the same time for examination. Then you ask yourself, 'How could I change this dynamic for the better?'

Be clear on what you and the other person need in the situation. Get beneath the behaviour to the intention, the need. Think about what they need from you – the words, the energy, the actions that will help them in this situation. How could you take the first step to improve the relationship? This third position gives you that insight.

The beauty of this exercise is that you can do it fast and you can do it anywhere. If you have a tricky meeting coming up you can take time during the days before it to take the perspective of others who are going to be at the meeting before you get in the room with them, whether it's doing some background research via colleagues or search engines or finding out from the horse's mouth what they are thinking. Try it. You will quickly be hooked when you see the empathy, understanding, success and influence this simple set of steps can give you and it will become a key part of your toolkit.

Extend Yourself: Build Trust and Connection

Appreciation is a wonderful thing.
It makes what is excellent in others belong to us as well.
VOLTAIRE, WRITER, DRAMATIST AND POET

The third rule of leveller is to extend yourself. To get on the *level* with others. To connect. To 'reach out' to borrow the US expression. Ultimately the success or failure of any situation you are involved in has a lot to do with the spirit you bring to it, the mood you create. Rather than blaming others for a lacklustre dynamic find a way to consciously shift the mood yourself, whether it's with a smile, a story or a question.

Extending yourself is a highly gravitas behaviour. A friend of mine once met former US president Jimmy Carter. Her name was also Carter and she was acting as his PR on a trip to the UK. She was intimidated by the formal diplomatic environment and found her voice and hands shaking uncharacteristically. Jimmy Carter must have noticed because he instantly put her at her ease. Noting her surname, he was full of questions about her family and where she was from. His interest was so genuine that she happily told him about her childhood, the house she'd been brought up in and where her parents lived. Then she got on with her job, setting him up for a press interview and thought nothing more about her nervousness.

Two days later her mother received a letter from Jimmy Carter saying how proud they must be of their daughter and what a credit she was to them. They still have that letter. This was a man with all the time-pressure excuses in the world for not paying attention but he made the time to show appreciation. If you appreciate someone they will remember how you made them feel for years after.

The Science of Extending Yourself

Be kind, for everyone you meet is fighting a hard battle.
PLATO, PHILOSOPHER

The effect of appreciation is far more than skin deep. It's hormonal. Paul Zak (see page 117) found via tests on volunteers (he's since been nicknamed the Vampire Economist for his love of blood tests) in his lab that 'When one person extends himself to another in a trusting way, the person being trusted experiences a surge in oxytocin ... the feeling of being trusted makes a person more trustworthy. Which over time makes people more inclined to trust ... which in turn ...'[6] In other words being an appreciative leveller has a hormonal effect – infectious in the nicest way. And when you understand that oxytocin not only boosts trust and drives empathy and connection, but that it also – crucially for the gravitas equation – damps down anxiety, you see that oxytocin, which Zak nicknames the moral molecule, could also be nicknamed the gravitas molecule.

Trust opens you up, stress closes you down. The difference between a surge of oxytocin and a surge of adrenalin is the difference between an environment where people listen to each other and trust is built, and where people compete. When people are stressed and adrenal, listening is difficult. High stress blocks oxytocin release and triggers adrenalin. It becomes more about them and us. The gremlins show up and it all goes pear-shaped. Oxytocin creates the *we* where ideas are shared and agreements reached. Being the person who can take a room from anxiety and judgement to openness and relaxed appreciation of each other – that's true soft power. This is not a power that comes as a result of the job you have, but a power that comes because people trust you, like you and believe in you. This kind of power lasts longer than any job.

Now, of course, no sane adult would say that being trusting all the time is wise. As Zak points out, it would be like walking around with a 'Kick me' sign on your back. As far as is wise take the advice of the Russian proverb: 'Trust, but verify'.

Try This: Extend Yourself

The key to the presence of sameness or difference is appreciation, and the means to make it real-life symphony is congruent communication.
VIRGINIA SATIR, FAMILY THERAPIST

The practices that follow are key to extending yourself and *levelling* with others. They will help you build an open, trusting environment.

People are Your Mirror – Go First

Extending yourself means taking responsibility for your effect on the world. A good belief to hold is that the people you meet are often your mirror. If you want friendliness – go first. If you can show them warmth or appreciation, you often get some back. When you meet people again that you've struggled to get along with in the past it's good to find a really natural smile when seeing them. (It can help to imagine you are smiling at someone you really do like. It switches on the true Duchenne smile in the eyes, rather than the tenser smile we do with the mouth.)

The Feeling of a Hug

Dr Paul Zak recommends that to maximise oxytocin – the hormone of extending yourself, of care and connection – we ideally need at least eight hugs a day. When this is not possible (i.e. in most professional life) Zak's advice to stimulate oxytocin is to rub your fingertips just between your ribs (try just below where the ribs separate at the front of your chest) to stimulate the vagus nerve. This nerve is rich in oxytocin receptors and stimulating it will help you to feel relaxed and safe, slowing down your heart rate and decreasing blood pressure. If you're in the heat of a debate even imagining the feeling of a hug from someone you love might trigger some of the good hormones and minimise the anxiety.

Relax Your Eyes: Find Open Focus

Eyes matter too. Levellers don't have a hunted look – they have warm relaxed eyes that relax others. If you want to be a leveller you need to learn how to relax your eyes, even under pressure.

The hunted look (where your eyes narrow and there is a sense of tension and focus) has been studied by psychologist Les Fehmi. His research shows that when stress is triggered our eyes narrow slightly into stressful 'narrow-beam attention'. Nature designed this narrow focus for fight or flight to help you find the exit or a weapon to get you out of trouble. Narrow-beam attention triggers the body into alert and it is only good for gravitas if the clock is ticking and you have a serious deadline or an important task to complete. In moments where you need to engage others and to build goodwill it does you no good at all. We read the tension in your eyes and we see the anxiety. Our own anxiety is triggered and it all goes a little gremlin-shaped.

Instead Fehmi advises 'open focus' as a way to calm the system down and pay attention in a more mindful way. Open focus is the kind of attention you have when we are at ease. Our eyes are relaxed. We take in the world around us. We feel loose, fluid and our eyes are soft rather than out on stalks. To find 'open focus' relax your face and find peripheral vision by seeing what is all around you as if you are standing on the top of a hill and can see for miles in all directions (imagining it is fine if you're in a small space). Close your eyes and feel the eyes drop into the back of the skull. When you open your eyes let the world come to you slowly and take it all in. Feel your eyes soften and relax and your state shift. This is great for leveller lightness and connection. A warm, relaxed smile in the eyes, as long as it is genuinely felt, can change everything for the better. It's infectious in the best way.[7]

Principle 6: Keep an Open Mind and a Level Head Toolkit

Power is the ability to act as if you can make happen, whatever it is that you want to make happen, knowing that you cannot, and being able to work with whatever does happen.

ELEANOR ROOSEVELT, FIRST LADY OF USA

Recognise the Gremlins

Take time to notice the gremlins. The blamer, placator, computer and distractor show up in life. Notice the patterns in yourself and others. If you see the pattern you can do something about it.

Be a Leveller Not a Gremlin

When the gremlins show up do something to improve the situation. Take responsibility. Sometimes if you want a situation to improve you have to be the hero not the victim and trust that the world will reflect the change back. If you want other people to be less irritable you need to make the change first. If you notice that others are stressed or jumpy, calm yourself down. If you said something you thought was innocuous and the person has reacted strongly was there something in your tone you were unconscious of?

Remember the leveller behaviours and practise these tips to help you with them:

- **Set yourself free – Name don't blame** Don't wind people up with blaming and inflaming, avoid the 'Why do you always?' and 'You're just like your father'-type comments. It's possible to name the emotion you're feeling without making it someone else's fault. Avoid tone that expresses contempt – it's a killer for relationships. Try to see the one good thing in that person and connect to them on that level.
- **Walk a mile in their shoes – Read the intention** Look beneath the surface to understand the fear, anxiety or loneliness driving bad behaviour and see if you can give what is needed rather than respond with knee-jerk negativity. Ask yourself what's the context? What's the pattern? Negative behaviour then just becomes information. You step back, see the context, depersonalise and your gravitas and authority ramps up because you can stay level-headed under pressure.
- **Extend yourself – Make me feel important**

> *I made a game of trying to make people talk about whatever they were interested in and learning as much as I could about their particular subject ... the interest is there lurking in every person. You only have to seek for it. It will make every encounter a challenge and it will keep alive one of the most valuable qualities a person has – curiosity.*
>
> ELEANOR ROOSEVELT, FIRST LADY OF THE USA

A simple way to remember to extend yourself is to borrow the Dale Carnegie principle to imagine that everyone you meet has a sign above their head that says 'Make me feel important'. Make people feel appreciated. Everyone wants that, however confident they seem.

Remember the Golden Rule
Lighten up and don't take things personally.

Principle 7: Get Results

The Mirror, Signal, Manoeuvre of Success

Our actions at any given moment do not depend only on the situation in which we find ourselves at that instant, but also on everything we have experienced and our future expectations ... each of our actions takes place in a temporal perspective; it depends on our temporal horizon at the precise moment of its occurrence.

PAUL FRAISSE, PSYCHOLOGIST

Results. No point having gravitas if you don't get them. Of course, if everything always went to plan and people always did what you asked them to do results would be easy. But it doesn't and they don't.

Chance definitely favours the prepared mind, but on its own preparation isn't enough. You also have to be able to respond. Marcus Aurelius gives clear advice for getting the result you want: 'In your actions let there be a willing promptitude, yet a regard for the common interest; due deliberation, yet no irresolution.' When it comes to results you have to find this precise balance – between 'willing promptitude' and the canny deliberation, the stubborn resolution that pushes you on to the finish line. Find this balance and you will get results.

To find both your promptitude and your resolution you need two kinds of time. Firstly you need what the Greeks called *chronos* – clock time. Then you need *kairos* – your ability to be in the present. The *results system* we will look at balances making a clear plan for the future (using *chronos*) and then responding to what happens in the present (using *kairos*). Time is a central feature of the results system as it was for ancient Greek wrestlers and orators alike when it came to getting a successful result.

Timing – the Foundation of a Great Result

*Observe due measure, for right timing is
in all things the important factor.*

HESIOD, POET

If you want results and you want to achieve them with gravitas, confidence and influence then you need to be able to make time work for you. Let's look at *chronos* and *kairos* in more detail in the table below.

	Chronos – Clock Time	*Kairos* – Your Ability to Be in the Present
Kind of Time	Clock time – timetables, alarm clocks, stopwatches, measurement of time.	In the moment – no sense of past or future, just one big now. Thinking on your feet.
Characterised By	Feeling of being organised, deadline and diary focused. Able to see time as linear. To think strategically through past and present.	A clear focus, total absorption, loss of self-consciousness and immediate sensory feedback. Feeling of ability to meet challenges. Sense of control and reward.
When it Works	*Chronos* allows you to schedule and organise your life. Great when organising matters more than building relationships.	*Kairos* allows you to live for the moment. Great when you need to be present to people or creative. You read situations and spot opportunities.

Start to pay attention to these different kinds of time. Notice where and how they show up. Who do you know who is precise about timekeeping and diarising (*chronos*) but has trouble being spontaneous and responsive? Who do you know who is great at thinking on their feet and being in the moment (*kairos*) but is frequently late and often unprepared?

Know your own strengths and build on them. Even more importantly, develop the kind of time that is weaker in you.

If you need more *chronos* practice make time to think ahead. Plan days, weeks and months ahead with the help of wall-planners, week-per-view diaries and smartphone calendars. Visualise how you want to feel in the meeting or presentation or whatever you are planning for. What would you want if it was today? Then think through step by step what you need to do to get there.

Giving yourself mini deadlines along the way can help enormously. The word resolution comes from the Latin *resolutionem*, meaning the process of reducing things into simpler forms. It's useful to keep this in mind when you set yourself a goal. The writer Anne Lamott tells the story of her 10-year-old brother when he was faced by the daunting prospect of trying to complete a report on birds in 24 hours that he'd had three months to do. Lamott describes the scene: 'And as he sat at the kitchen table, close to tears, immobilised by the hugeness of the task ahead … Then my father sat down beside him, put his arm round my brother's shoulder and said, "Bird by bird buddy. Just take it bird by bird."'[1]

Brushing up on *kairos* involves developing your ability to be totally present to the moment. One simple way is to tune into your senses. See what you see, feel what you feel, hear what you hear. Look at something around you that you have never noticed before. Go back to the FOFBOC exercise (see page 30).

Once you've understood the core difference between *chronos* and *kairos* then you need to know how to use them to get the results you want with gravitas.

The Results System – the Mirror, Signal, Manoeuvre of Gravitas

The system we're going to look at next will get you results. It's a keystone of the dynamism and wisdom of gravitas – the balance between the 'willing promptitude' and 'no irresolution' that Marcus Aurelius speaks of. It's the mirror, signal, manoeuvre of gravitas and you can apply it to pretty much *any* challenge. It takes you through step by step from planning in *chronos* to the moment you face your audience in *kairos*.

The system is simple:

Intention (*chronos*) + attention (*kairos*) = Result

- **Intention (*chronos*)** Think about preparing for a tricky meeting with someone. First you set your intention. You get into *chronos*. You think into the future and you plan the steps you need to take to get there. You do the work knowing that the more you prepare, the better your chances of success.
- **Attention (*kairos*)** With your preparation done you get present. This is crucial. You have to let go trusting that you have done enough. In the moment whether you are faced by an audience of one or a thousand your focus needs to be on them. You give them your full attention rather than fretting about how you're doing. Make sure you are relaxed and focused so you can get into the pure presence of *kairos* in the communication and respond as the situation changes, always with your goal in mind.
- **Result** This sequence of intention (*chronos*) and attention (*kairos*) is key to achieving the *result* you want. On their own they're no good. All *chronos* makes you stiff and overly analytical. All *kairos* makes you a little fluffy and unstructured.

Excellence in any field, from politics to sport, demands you find the balance between your planning in *chronos* and your presence in *kairos*. When you find the balance you create the right conditions for gravitas to break through.

If you want a good example of how preparation combines with the boldness and bravery to let your instincts take over, look no further than Martin Luther King (see box, below).

'I Have a Dream'

Martin Luther King's 1963 'I Have a Dream' speech is a great example of how the alchemy of a prepared mind meeting the needs of the moment is often the key to greatness. The 'I have a dream' section wasn't in the written speech. It was in King's consciousness. He had long been talking about a dream of seeing little 'negro boys and girls walking to school with little white boys and girls, playing in the parks together and going swimming together'. King had even made a speech about the dream in Detroit earlier that year but he thought he wouldn't have time in this speech on jobs and freedom to include it.

For the first 12 minutes or so he stuck to the speech he had stayed up to write by hand the night before. Then King paused for a moment and took in the thousands of people in front of him and 'All of a sudden' he explained after, 'this thing came to me that I'd used many times before, that thing about having a dream – and I just felt that I wanted to use it here.' And so he started 'I say to you today, my friends, though, even though we face the difficulties of today and tomorrow, I still have a dream.'

So that you can apply the results system in your life, let's think through it step by step.

Intention

Our plans miscarry because they have no aim.
When a man does not know what harbour he is
making for, no wind is the right wind.

SENECA, ROMAN STATESMAN, PHILOSOPHER AND DRAMATIST

Intentions matter massively to gravitas. Your intention is the harbour you're sailing for. If you are clear on where you're headed – a successful pitch or a friendly chat, for example – then you'll be much more likely to get there. No matter what life throws your way you'll be able to adjust your sails.

Psychologist Philip Zimbardo suggests that *chronos* is key to getting a clear intention and a good result. The ability to travel through time in your mind helps you gather confidence and motivation, so key to success in most situations. You can think of past experiences that give you confidence (or taught you a useful lesson) or future visions that inspire or spur you to action.

First, Zimbardo says, you need high levels of 'positive past' – good memories that give you confidence and minimise anxiety. Then you also need 'moderately high positive future' – your confidence and boldness to try new things are inspired by your vision of a good result.[2] Stand-up comedians will tell you that they get a good result if they visualise success rather than failure. If they visualise the audience laughing at their jokes it makes it far easier to prepare and walk out on stage. You may also want to step briefly into negative past to draw learning where it will illuminate your goal. However, if it won't illuminate it don't go there – stick with positive past.

Outcome Setting

Good intentions are paved by your values. When you are starting to get clear on what you want remember that the best goals build on your strengths and feel true to your values – they are guided by that inner north star (see page 31). So make sure you set outcomes that feel challengingly exciting rather than ones that fill you with dull, dark dread. Know the difference and choose accordingly.

It can help to ask yourself:

1. What do I want to achieve in this situation?
2. Who are my audience and what do they need from me?
3. What's our common purpose?
4. When I achieve this result what will success look like?
5. What obstacles or challenges are there to achieving the best result?
6. What steps do I need to take to ensure I overcome them?
7. What lessons can I learn from similar things I have done in the past that I can apply?

Set Implementation Intentions

When you've set your intention the next step is to set clear milestones on the road to the big goal. These milestones work best when they are accompanied by what are called 'implementation intentions'. What that means is that the goals are something you see, hear and feel happening in the future. This comes from the work of psychologist Peter Gollwitzer, whose work focuses on how we motivate and self-regulate ourselves. Gollwitzer says that if we imagine clearly what we will do in a specific situation the actions in the moment are easier because we've already set the intention.[3] See what you will look like when you rehearse. Feel what it will feel like when it's done and you're drinking a glass of wine. These milestones help you get the result.

Diarise and Delegate: This is the next step. What do I need to do and when to get me to my goal? List the actions and the deadlines, get them in your diary. Delegate what needs to be done to the people who need to do it.

Get on Track

If you want an example of someone who makes it happen, with a blend of intention and attention, *chronos* and *kairos*, meet Paulette Randall. Below she explains how she sets her focus as a director. She talks about how she takes time to think and set clear goals, how she balances a clear intention and resolution with focused attention in the moment. When you think that she was responsible for much of the directing of the London Olympics Opening Ceremony in 2012, with its cast of thousands, you know that this advice has been crash-tested.

My confidence comes from knowing that I have prepped myself for what I'm about to do and giving myself time to think. You have to take the time to think, 'What is it I'm trying to create? What's the feeling I want?' There's always time. When people say I haven't got time, it's actually about prioritising, it's about time management. People make the mistake of thinking that taking time to think is a waste of time. And it's not, it's a brilliant use of your time. Because if you don't make time to think all you have is knee-jerk reactions.

You have to trust that it's going to get to where it's going to get to. I know that I work backwards – I know that opening night – I've got to hit that. There's no way I can do what I do and not fulfil. I have to get everyone ready for that first night, for that stage. Working backwards you go, so the last week is about all those run-throughs and notes. Before you get there you should be running it. There are certain things you have to do – and that's fine, because once you know where you're going you can plan accordingly. Then you have to pay attention to whether you're on track and adjust accordingly.

You have to allow yourself to respond – to be there for the people you're working with. You don't know quite how they are going to do it. You've got your way of directing and getting them there, but their personal journeys are always going to be different. You have to allow space for that in a way. Your job is being an enabler – to create a place where you should be able to play and never feel stupid. That empowers people because no one can ever ask a stupid question.

Attention – How to be Present and Focused

Our acts of voluntary attending, as brief and fitful
as they are, are nevertheless momentous and critical,
determining us as they do, to higher or lower destinies.
WILLIAM JAMES, PHILOSOPHER AND PSYCHOLOGIST

Once you have a clear intention, and a plan to get there, the next step is attention. After the careful planning of *chronos* comes the presence to your audience of *kairos*; in this balance is gravitas.

The essential point to grasp about the attention that *kairos* requires is that it's not all about you. *Attention to others is what counts.* The clue's in the word *communication.* It comes from the Latin word *communis,* to make common, to share. Communication is what happens in the spaces between people. *Kairos* is about getting you firmly into those spaces. This attention to others is a magic wand for communication. I've seen it help people win pitches, get jobs and make massive professional steps up. Why? Because it allows you to lose self-consciousness. It becomes about *we* rather than *I*. You merge with others. This is what Marcus Aurelius describes when he says 'Things push and pull on each other, and breathe together, and are one.'

If you ask any sporting hero what's in their head in a game the answer is 'Nothing'. When your focus is firmly on the ball rather than in your worries you'll be most likely to hit it successfully when it comes hurtling your way. We can all learn from their focus and their ease.

Get in the Zone

Michael Parker is both an ex-Olympic hurdler and a former Saatchi's advertising man. He is now a very-much-in-demand pitch coach. When we spoke, Parker pointed out that when it comes to results, ease is key – getting yourself to a point where instinct can take over and guide you.

When you look at the great athletes you see a sense of control and awareness. To be seriously competitive you need a way to get rid of extraneous stuff from your head – to be in the zone. The very first time I took part in the Olympics I ended up afterwards realising I'd been so focused I could not tell you if the stadium had been empty or full. You're never going to not have nervous energy, but you control it. You manage the hormones of fear of flight. Your aim is to get to the point where something else takes over. When you're at the top of your game in training you manage the emotional side, the adrenalin, so you don't overdo it. It's now or never. You get a massive, massive rush before the gun goes off, and then you go. Everything hangs in that moment.

That's why as an athlete I spent a great deal of time practising how to be totally relaxed. That's when the inner game comes together – when an inner sense of calm and self-confidence descends at the start of the race.

Kairos in Action

'I've worked so hard, I just don't understand why I'm not getting selected.' Anna was a candidate for political selection. Time after time she travelled up to distant constituencies to present herself as their perfect candidate to put forward as the party's MP at election time. Selections are daunting – designed to test a candidate's mettle. The candidate comes into a room full of party members – sometimes 80 or more people. They present themselves and then answer questions about their political views and commitment to the constituency.

Anna was too focused on herself. She'd forgotten about her audience. As a result she gabbled, as if she was downloading the words rather than having a conversation with the audience. Anna needed to go from looking on at herself *camera-in* to looking *camera-out* at her audience with care, compassion and curiosity. As soon as she shifted her focus, remembering that they were just as nervous about choosing the wrong candidate, she softened and her natural authority and presence entered the building. A week later she emailed to say 'We did it! Last night I went to my selection interview and I got selected to a winnable seat!'

Result: How to Think on Your Feet

> *No plan survives contact with the enemy.*
> HELMUTH VON MOLTKE, FIELD MARSHAL

> *Everyone has a plan until they get punched in the mouth.*
> MIKE TYSON, BOXER

In the words of Sir Lawrence Freedman, professor of war studies at King's College London, 'The point about good strategy is not that it follows formula, but that it draws on a shrewd understanding of the possibilities inherent in the moment, and how they might be realised.'[4] This section gives you that understanding and it means that in the heat of the moment you have all the 'willing promptitude' and resolution you need for your gravitas to kick in when you need it most.

I used to work with an ex-SAS survival trainer. He said the first thing they teach you in combat is 'When you come under fire, breathe. If you don't breathe, you can't think, and if you can't think, you're dead.'

This powerful piece of advice takes us into the single most important piece of advice for getting results. The result, whether you're on

Centre Court at Wimbledon or in a high-stakes negotiation, is about what happens in the moment. How you think on your feet, even when as Mike Tyson said, you've just been punched in the mouth. What you need for those high-stakes moments, where the result hangs in the balance, is what psychologist and mindfulness and kung fu expert Dr Tamara Russell calls the 'big now'.

The big now allows you to take hold of time and to carve out a moment to get your thoughts clear. Time to think. When the pressure hits you get a grip. The big now means that you think on your feet, fast, and find that fine balance between what Marcus Aurelius calls 'due deliberation, yet no irresolution'. Then you have true grace under fire – the true test of gravitas.

Here's an example of the big now. One of my clients was in the middle of a major TV interview on the importance of financial education when the broadcaster asked her what the acronym APR (annual percentage rate) stood for. Brain-freeze hit and the words vanished, even though, as she said in the green room after, two minutes before the interview she could have told you in a flash. Luckily we'd practised the breathing a few weeks before. It came back to her and in that moment she did exactly the right thing. Rather than let the tension and fear curl her up into a little ball, hedge-hog-like, she breathed down into the fear. She let the terror pass, she breathed it out. Then she waited for a relaxed breath to come back. She still couldn't remember what APR stood for so she changed tack, telling the broadcaster why it mattered. 'Good save' said the interviewer later, and she was invited back. None of the friends and family watching her interview even noticed the mistake.

If you'd like to be able to find the same poise, to come across with gravitas and get the result, here's how to take control of time.

The Art of the Big Now

When force of circumstance upsets your equanimity,
lose no time in recovering your self-control and do not remain
out of tune longer than you can help. Habitual recurrence
to the harmony will increase your mastery of it.
MARCUS AURELIUS, ROMAN EMPEROR AND PHILOSOPHER

The big now is about your heart and your brain. You'll have noticed that you can't think clearly if you're not calm. The ancient world noticed too. For the Greeks the heart was the source of resourcefulness. Control of the heart meant control of the whole system.[5]

Recent research from the Institute of HeartMath in the USA backs up this heart–resourcefulness connection. Research into 'cardiac coherence' shows that keeping your head is a lot about keeping your heart rate under control. When you get stressed your heart rate goes haywire and this 'incoherent heart rhythm' affects your brain function, scrambling your thinking so you make stupid decisions and say the wrong thing. The answer is to get your heart rate coherent by calming yourself down via the breath. Essentially a coherent heart rate allows you to sound coherent to others.[6]

The best tip I've ever heard for how to find your big now came from a senior police officer in London's Metropolitan Police. An expert at dealing with aggression on London's streets, she told me that she'd learnt a crucial lesson at Hendon (the main training centre for the Metropolitan Police Service). 'If someone is aggressive, you give yourself a moment. You breathe out, let the anger go. You wait for the in-breath, you decide the tone you want and only then do you speak.' Using this technique helps the police to avoid emotional contagion. They notice their reaction to aggression, they breathe it out and let it go. Then they take in a cooler response. By waiting for the breath they allow the emotion to move on.

If you'd like to find your cool under pressure the Institute of HeartMath teaches this practical freeze-frame technique. You'll find it a powerful ally when stress rises.

Try This: Press Pause – the Freeze-frame Tool

If you are distressed by anything external the pain is not due to the thing itself but to your own estimate of it, and this you have the power to revoke at any moment. If the cause of the trouble lies in your own character, set about reforming your principles, who else is there to hinder you?

MARCUS AURELIUS, ROMAN EMPEROR AND PHILOSOPHER

The power of this technique is how it gives you 'impulse awareness' and 'impulse control' as they say in the science of emotion. You can defuse rather than ignite negative emotions effectively when you get the hang of it. It allows you to stay present and controlled.

1. Identify a stressful feeling. Notice what happens and how it makes you feel.
2. Press pause on this moment (like freezing the frame of a DVD).
3. Shift your focus to your heart area. Breathe in through your heart and out through your solar plexus. Imagine breathing out dark, negative emotion and breathing in light if it helps.
4. Self-generate a positive feeling such as appreciation or care.
5. Notice how this positive feeling changes your physical and emotional state.
6. Then think. This is the way things are, what do I want to do now? It can help to remind yourself. What is the common purpose? Who

am I here to serve? Who am I here to help? What will happen if I act? What will happen if I don't? How do we move this forward?

7. With that focus, speak from the heart. Be honest and keep the tone measured and controlled.

Clarify Your Purpose

Then come the hard choices. What do I believe?
To what extent am I prepared to live up to my beliefs?
How far am I ready to support them?

ELEANOR ROOSEVELT, FIRST LADY OF THE USA

When you're dealing with complex situations the trick is to remember who you're there for. When you are clear why you're there or who you're there for, it's easier to tune into resolution. In that big now you may make a tough decision. It doesn't have to make everyone happy to be the right choice.

The penny dropped for a client of mine in the public sector when she realised she was failing to protect the interests of the young people she was representing by not speaking up in meetings. She was protecting the wrong people. She needed to clarify her goals and keep the right people in the frame. This is about tapping into what's called *preventative compassion*. If you know that a decision being discussed is likely to cause problems in the future then it gives you a good reason to help and to drive through an outcome.

Above all, when it comes to getting results remember that, as any good sailor will tell you, you must set your course and then pay attention. Balance your camera-in – focus and clarity of purpose, with your camera-out – awareness of the world around you, you stand a good chance of getting the result you want.

Principle 7: Get Results Toolkit

With a balanced time perspective that learns from the past,
draws energy and emotion from the present, and is guided
by a clear vision for the future, each of us as individuals
and all of us as a world can accomplish great things.

PHILIP ZIMBARDO, PSYCHOLOGIST

Set Your Intention

First – *chronos.* What do you want and what are the steps you need to take to get there? Set a clear outcome that is achievable, measurable and pleasurably challenging. Break it down 'bird by bird'. Visualise your implementation steps and then get to work. Refine your skills through practice. This is key to gravitas in front of an audience as it allows you to be more instinctive. The skills need to be so deeply in the muscle via repetition that you don't have to think about them at all.

Focus Your Attention

Now for *kairos.* Kairos requires camera-out attention on the room. It can help to obey the 80/20 principle: 80 per cent attention for the room, a clear sensory focus on what you can see hear and feel out there. Then 20 per cent for your inner state – what you are feeling and thinking? A good question to get you into attention is 'How can I help?' Be compassionate and generous. Aim to relax and enjoy the activity to the point that awareness and activity merge and you lose all self-consciousness.

When You Come Under Fire, Breathe

If you need to think on your feet press pause, breathe and think, 'So this is happening. How do we move this forward?'

PART TWO

Gravitas in Action

The readiness is all.

WILLIAM SHAKESPEARE, *HAMLET*

Part Two is about *helping you flex your gravitas muscles with confidence* because, as we've discovered, gravitas is a mindset as much as anything else. The more you practise the principles we've covered, the better you will get at gravitas. In these chapters you will find tips, tricks and reminders to get you up and moving fast so that you are confident, poised and in control.

So now you need to roll your sleeves up and apply the principles in the world around you. Being brilliant in your bathroom doesn't really work when it comes to gravitas. Gravitas needs to meet the world – it's what you do with it that counts. All that knowledge, purpose and passion is wasted if you don't get out there and do something with it.

What you contribute via your knowledge, your purpose and your passion is up to you – it could be monumental or subtle, as circumstances and confidence dictate. You might make a presentation that changes the minds of your work colleagues and helps them commit to a new idea or you might win political office.

The Big Five

I'm going to focus on what I call the *big five: presentations and talks, meetings, telephone calls and teleconferences, interviews and pitches* and *on camera*. These are the most common professional spotlight situations – those moments where all eyes are on you and you need to impress. They are the snakes and ladders – get your spotlight moments right and you will gain the traction to rise in your career and life. As a coach I hear questions and insights about the big five almost every day in my working life, so I've gathered together for you the absolute essentials that help my clients excel in their spotlight situations.

In the following chapters I've gathered together the top tips that I've been passing on to clients for years. I've also interviewed broadcasters, performance poets, pitch coaches and interview experts to help you finesse your gravitas in challenging moments. Use these tips as a handy aide-memoire to pick up every time you need to practise.

You'll find that the Presentations and Talks chapter (see opposite) is the most detailed. In many ways it's the core set of steps for flexing your gravitas. Why? All of the big five are to some extent presentations. Whether you're in a meeting, in an interview, on a phone call or pitching you are presenting yourself – as such the core content in terms of structure and rehearsal is to be found in Presentations and Talks. The subsequent four sections adapt and tweak the advice for the different challenges so that you can subtly adjust your style for the requirements of each. Always keep the core system for presentations and talks in mind when planning and rehearsing content.

Presentations and Talks

The Audience is The Hero

The first rule of presenting with gravitas?

'You are not the hero. The audience is the hero.'

US CEO and author Nancy Duarte nails it.[1]

When it comes to presenting with gravitas, Duarte's *Star Wars* analogy is brilliant. As the presenter you are Yoda to the audience's Luke Skywalker. Your job is to be the wise mentor who equips the audience for their challenges so that they can transform, overcome their limitations and set out on their hero's journey, to borrow from mythology. Yes, even if they are the local finance team they get to be the hero and you get to be the mentor. You just dial the dramatics up or down depending on their expectations.

This has big implications for how you present. You don't need all that jazz or an overdose of charisma. Gravitas is stiller than that. Quite simply you need great content, focus, ease and real interest in the people who have come to listen to you.

But that doesn't mean presenting with gravitas is a walk in the park. Oh no. Gravitas requires that you provoke thinking. That you change minds. You need to know exactly who you are and what you offer (see Principle 1 on pages 23–42). Your content needs to be rich in thought and meaning (see Principle 3 on pages 63–83 for lots on this). And you need to engage your audience with energy, passion and authority (see Principle 5 on pages 105–120).

Plus, purpose is key. You have to be ambitious about your purpose. What will change because of what you say? Because if nothing changes when you present you have wasted the audience's time. People often say to this, 'But I'm updating my audience.' Yes, by all means update them, but make sure that the insight from the update changes something for them. A subtle change is fine; perhaps you cause them to have a small shift in belief or a more nuanced understanding.

And be ambitious for you. Don't think it's okay to deliver a generalised presentation on your subject area. People have come to see you. Deliver your take on the subject, express what insight you bring to it. Give the audience a new angle they haven't considered before.

Put the Present in Presentation

Chris Anderson, the founder of TED (see page 107), describes beautifully what makes presentations and talks powerful. He says, 'A successful talk is a little miracle – people see the world differently afterwards.'[2]

A good presentation should be a gift to the audience. Presentation. *Present*. Bit of a giveaway in language terms really. And when it comes to presenting what really matters to your gravitas, your confidence and your enjoyment is knowing that you have something good to offer.

Think about birthdays. That feeling of anticipation of knowing you have chosen something just right that the person will love. It's a very different feeling from handing over something hastily bought wrapped in a plastic bag.

Gravitas in presentation is the former; knowledge, purpose and passion carefully chosen and packaged for your audience. You don't overwhelm them with lots of cheap tat. You give them one small, thoughtfully chosen and beautifully wrapped gem that they can enjoy for many years to come.

Why? Because the belief 'this is useful for my audience' when you stand up to speak is essential. Before the presentation you can then enjoy a sense of anticipation of knowing what you have to give is good, even as the butterflies start to flutter in your stomach. And during the presentation you can enjoy it knowing that you are ready. You pay attention in a more relaxed way. Think of the easy energy of a great birthday party host who knows the party is perfectly prepared and planned, so they can relax and give their full attention to their guests.

If you've ever turned up to a presentation unprepared you will know the opposite experience. You become the harassed and unprepared host who rushes around frantically. If you are worried that you are wasting your audience's time it leaks out of you. The audience will sense your discomfort and uncertainty. You see them shift and you start to rush and overcompensate. But as soon as you feel safe in the knowledge that what you have to say is useful, everything works. You get into a dance with the audience, giving them what they need. They reciprocate with interest. Then, believe me, presentations can be enjoyable. You just have to put in the right amount of work.

Get Ready – How to Prepare Your Content

Gravitas and professional poise go hand in hand. Professionals prepare to the point where they can let go and enjoy the moment. Here's how to prepare, practise and deliver with real impact.

Walt Disney's animators used to say that there were three Walts, the dreamer, the realist and the spoiler, or critic. For them it was tricky – they never knew which version of the mercurial Disney was coming into a meeting. For the rest of us, it's very helpful – as the author and thinker Robert Dilts took these three sides of Disney, and turned them into a practical strategy for creativity.[3] When working on a presentation, it helps to go through each stage in turn.

> *Creativity as a total process involves the coordination of these three subprocesses: dreamer, realist and critic. A dreamer without a realist cannot turn ideas into tangible expressions. A critic and a dreamer without a realist just become stuck in a perpetual conflict. The dreamer and a realist might create things, but they might not achieve a high degree of quality without a critic. The critic helps to evaluate and refine the products of creativity.*
>
> ROBERT B. DILTS, *STRATEGIES OF GENIUS: VOLUME 1*

- The **dreamer** dreams big – **inspire** yourself.
- The **realist** makes it happen – **organise** yourself.
- The **critic** edits and refines until the content is audience-ready – **edit** yourself.

Dreamer – Inspire Yourself

Alfred Hitchcock, like Disney, was a believer in the power of dreaming big. Before the movie-maker started work on a new production he'd go and sit at the back of an empty cinema and 'watch' his own movie from start to finish. He dreamed up the project and then he went out and made it. I'd advise you to think this big when you plan a presentation. Get creative first then organise later.

The same strategy works well at the very beginning of your preparation.

---

1. Find a comfortable place to sit. Close your eyes and picture yourself sitting at the back of an auditorium. It's dark and there are rows of empty seats in front of you. When the lights come up you will see yourself on that screen doing your presentation exactly as you planned. See it, hear it, feel it. Make it bright, appealing and exactly how you want it to be. It can take as long as you like to get the movie just right and you can go back to it as much as you want.

2. Replay that movie reel in your head as you write down any ideas and phrases that come to you. Ask yourself, what excites me? What would I enjoy sharing with my audience? What are the ideas I want them to remember? What drives me to share this information with my audience? Make your notes as visual and colourful as possible. The trick is to start from a really good feeling – it's going to be the energy that allows you to prepare in a professional and thorough way and in a way that is – crucially – also fun.

3. Once you've got the core ideas, create a storyboard to record key images and ideas. It can be on a pinboard or in a notebook. You can add newspaper articles or images that inspire you. This is a process of pulling all the ideas in. Then the realist can organise them (see below). If you know how to use mind maps (and if you don't look at Tony Buzan's tips for mind-mapping on www.buzanworld.com), they are also a great way to make patterns and connections.

Realist – Organise Yourself

Now, time to get real. Time to focus on the audience.

You have your thoughts gathered together on a storyboard or mind map but they are currently ordered in a way that only makes sense to you. The job of a good presenter is to structure the material in a way that helps the audience understand it too. You need to – going back to the empathy principles in Principle 6 (see page 135) – put yourself in their shoes. Making them the hero requires that you know the difference between their understanding and yours and set out to bridge this gap in a way that helps them engage and understand.

These heroes in your presentation movie – who are they? What do they want/need? And in what order?

1. Research

Go back to the empathy exercise in Principle 6 and take time to walk in the shoes of your audience (see page 134). Do some Internet research or talk to people if you can. Find out about what they want and need. It's key to putting the present back in presentation. Note that the more senior your audience the more crucial it is that you do this. Very senior audiences want the absolute distillation of your message. No flannel, just the facts, focused for them. The more you can canvas their exact requirements, the more likely you are to hit the mark.

2. Focus your thinking

Now answer these questions:

- What's the problem you want to help the audience solve?
- What's at stake here? Why should they commit to and care about this? What's in it for them?
- What was the insight that helped you understand this problem?
- What insights do you have that they'd benefit from? (One of the real secrets to successful presenting is to give away really brilliant diamond insights. Don't be a hoarder, be generous about sharing your golden nuggets of insight. It's the best way to get others to talk about your work. It's also good for your creativity as you have to dream up new ideas.)
- What information can you give that is scarce or valuable? (This makes you credible.)
- What statistics or examples do you have that will make you a trusted adviser? How can you back up your facts?

- What questions or objections might the audience have to your ideas? What's the elephant in the room – that everyone's aware of but no one will mention? What will worry or frighten them – deep down – even if they won't say it to you? How can you calm those fears? How can you address and reframe their concerns?
- What is the core idea you want them to take away?
- What are the tools they need to be able to do this?
- What are the stories or insights you can share with them to bring this alive?
- Where do they need you to begin?
- Where do you want to end?

When you've answered all of these questions see if you can (and it will take a little thought) cook them down into a one-line summary of your angle on the subject that you have to present on. This is hard to do but when you get that line the presentation becomes crystal clear in your mind.

3. Organise your structure

The amount of time this takes really depends on how much time you have. If it's a big speech there's a real luxury in starting to think about it with the space of a few months. Then you can really pull ideas together.

You're going to need a big sheet of paper (ideally poster sized) and Post-it notes for this.

We're going to use the classic *message map* structure to hang the talk on. It draws on the work of Professor Alan Monroe around motivation. It's a simple structure that allows you to lay out a message in a way that is clear and visual, and that takes you from the problem to the solution. Our brains like to problem solve and this structure of challenge to resolution fits the dramatic arc that we looked at in

Principle 5 (see page 116). The reason I like it is that it takes you on a hero's journey – a classic narrative arc from challenge, to transforming insight, to reminding the audience of what's in it for them so that they commit. If you want to know more on this I highly recommend Nancy Duarte's brilliant book *Resonate* (Wiley, 2010). It takes you through examples of world-class speeches using the hero's journey structure.

Doing a message map can actually be quite fun. The map example below shows you the structure. Mark out the four quadrants on the sheet of paper and put the appropriate heading in each quadrant, following the map.

You have two options now. Take your work from dreamer (see page 170) and either write ideas directly on to the message map in the sections that they fit best, or, and this is my preference, take Post-it notes and stick them in the sections. Then you can move them around and edit as you refine the message.

1. Problem

- What's the challenge your audience are facing? What do they want to escape from?
- Why is solving the problem important and what will it be like for them when the problem is solved?
- Make sure you frame the problem in a way that keeps the audience's spirits high.
- Any problem can be framed positively: 'Nice weather for ducks' over 'What a gloomy day'.

2. Solution/Transforming Insight

- What can you offer as ideas to move the audience forward?
- What have your transformational insights been when struggling with the problem yourself? It's a good point to disclose something from your own life here – to build connection with the audience.
- This is a good place to tell your story about your diamond insight.

3. How To – What's in it for the audience?

- Here help the audience to understand how they should commit to the ideas. Give them practical steps and also motivate them as to why it matters and what's in it for them. Give examples of how they have helped you or others.

- This is a section that can stretch in terms of time (speech coach KC Baker calls it the accordion section for that reason). You can have five minutes of practical ideas in a short presentation or 40 minutes in a workshop.

4. Call to Action – What's next?

- What are the action steps you want the audience to take?

- If the context of your presentation is a professional one, make the call to action very clear. Do you want them to sell your idea for you in the wider world? To connect you with people or make things happen? To influence tricky people? To help you move the idea forward creatively?

- Know what you want, make it crystal clear to your audience and make it achievable. It can help to describe a future vision as if it's already happening: 'Wouldn't it be great … to be sitting in … to be able to say …' etc.

At this stage aim for at least three pieces of content per quadrant: points, stories, examples or statistics that will form the building blocks of your talk. So you'll have about 12 pieces of core content across the four quadrants of the map. If the presentation is short you won't use all of them – the critic will cut many of them (see overleaf). But the point is to be able to choose the right ideas for this audience. Get the big rocks in first; you can put the smaller details into the talk later.

At this stage it can help to sit down with a voice recorder and record the content that you have so far (keep it loose and chatty – a very rough draft). Listen to it and see what you like. See what flows. See what sticks. Write down what works. And where you falter, alter.

Make a Store of Your Stories

My tip – to save you time in future keep all your stories, themes and ideas. You can either take a photo of the Post-its/ message map/storyboard as a record or store them as notes in a notebook or digitally. The stories you come up with can be a resource for you in different talks with different audiences. If you have a store of stories you'll find that you can pull together presentations and talks quickly, and with a flavour that is all yours. This is key to really giving the audience what Nancy Duarte calls a STAR moment – Something They'll Always Remember. One of the paradoxes of presenting is that the more you can tell a story that is specific and has real meaning to you (a feeling of safe disclosure is what you're aiming for) the more it resonates with your audience on a general level.

Critic – Edit

For a talk to be brilliant it need not be interminable. Have you ever heard an audience say that a presentation was too short? Crisp, clear and concise is a gift – and a test of a good mind.

That's why the critic's job is essential. Critics cut. They crystallise. Clarify. Distil. Or in scientific terms: to go from divergent creative thinking – the brainstorm, to focused convergent thinking – where all your thinking starts to focus on one point.

Focused, pared down and elegant is the aim. The more pared down it is the more powerful. Think about presents – the gem in the small, beautiful box is so much better than thousands of knick-knacks.

The critic thinks carefully about what the audience need and in what order. The critic is aware of possible objections and worries the audience might have and has the boldness to acknowledge them in advance.

Think of the TV news. News is memorable. That's because news-readers understand that repetition is essential to good storytelling.

- **Intro** *They tell you what they're going to tell you.* The newsreader gives you the headlines.
- **Core content** *Then they tell you it.* You hear each of the stories in the order that the headlines were given.
- **Wrap** *Then they tell you what they've told you.* You hear the headlines again, although they may be presented in a slightly different way.

You already have lots of *core content* – it's what you've created in your message map. Now you need to create the *intro* and the *wrap*. Give the audience the frame of your presentation in the intro on which they can hang the information on, deliver the core content and then wrap it up in a way that they can remember.

Think of this stage as the first draft of your talk. Take a new sheet of paper. Write in bullet points. Avoid long sentences and paragraphs – short is good for speech as we learned in Principle 3 (see page 73).

- **Intro** Welcome, thank and make the audience the hero.
- **Core content** Content from the message map (problem, solution, how to and call to action).
- **Wrap** Sum up. Reprise your call to action and main themes (repetition is needed if they are to remember). Add a question or quote. Send the audience off inspired.

Once you've been through the dreamer, realist and critic stages you have all you need to do the really important preparation for the speech – *practising*. Writing a talk is not preparation for speaking with gravitas. It prepares the knowledge aspect of your talk – but not the passion. And as we learned in Principle 5 (see pages 105–120), passion is key. So practise is what we're going to do next.

Get Set – How to Practise

The problem for most people when it comes to presentation? The dread of the event itself puts them off rehearsal. They find it easier to go into deep denial. Yet practice is your greatest ally when it comes to overcoming nerves. It allows you to get the content learnt so deeply that you can relax and – yes – enjoy the experience of presenting.

The speakers that you admire rehearse. They rehearse to the point that they make it look easy. Steve Jobs used to rehearse for hours on his big speeches. He knew that it was the secret to easy authority on stage. What fine-distinction actors understand about rehearsal is that its aim is exploration. Yes, you learn what comes in what order so you can move smoothly through your content. But it's also about learning more about what you want to say, finding the expressions that really work for you and the stories that bring your presentation alive. Treat rehearsal as exploration and it becomes far more enjoyable.

Practice really needn't be a big deal. It can happen in lots of ways and in lots of places. Practice means saying it or thinking about saying it. This can be anywhere, any time.

Refine and Record

Start gently. Take your one page of bullet points and a device that you can record yourself on. Record yourself speaking your introduction. Listen back to it. Tweak your written text until it is what you actually want to say (often surprisingly different to what you wrote down at first). Record yourself again. Listen to it as if you were in the audience and add any missing pieces.

Do the same set of steps with the core content and the wrap. By the time you have recorded and listened back to yourself a few times you start to find that the content is in the muscle. It's a deceptively easy way to rehearse because you can do it sitting on the sofa with a cup of tea. But by the time you've finished you have a presentation that is really yours. In the muscle. It's a fantastic foundation for confidence.

Walk Your Talk

The next stage is to – literally – walk your talk. To learn it to the point where it is conversational it can help to walk around the house and speak it until it feels smooth. Or if time is tight walk the talk through in your mind as you go to work. Above all what you're refining are the segues. Smooth links between ideas show a real mastery of your thinking. They also keep you calm and graceful as you don't have to fumble around in your memory for the next point. You can be really flexible, dynamic and immediate in your delivery: stop to answer a question, start a story, digress (*digressio* – a favourite trick of Cicero's) and then come back to the end, with the audience hanging on your every word. Of course, delivery this pithy and powerful requires you to have your thinking ordered, sequenced and memorised.

A Note About Slides

This is not a book about good presentation slides – look at *Presentation Zen* by Garr Reynolds (New Riders, 2007) and *slide:ology* (O'Reilly Media, 2008) by Nancy Duarte if you want to know more about this.

My sole message to you with regards to slides is that the audience came to see *you*, not your slides. Your slides will help them to understand and remember your words but they are in service to you and should be clear and simple and kept to a minimum. Arguably if you want true gravitas you can do without them. If you do decide to use them make sure you practise how you present them. *Never, never, never* read off your slides. They are for the audience not you. Your script must be clear in your head so that you can present without them. Indeed you should cue each slide verbally. In news the audio always comes slightly before the visual. If you want gravitas follow the same principle. It makes you seem clear and ordered in your thinking and on top of your brief.

Be Your Own Coach

As you start to feel like you have the material at your fingertips practise in front of the mirror so you can see yourself. The Greek orator Demosthenes swore by it. Or record yourself on video. Then you can be your own coach. If you can bear it, it gives you good feedback. You'll see exactly what works and what needs to be changed. Chances are you'll also be pleasantly surprised by how much better it looks than it seems inside your head.

You may feel that watching yourself isn't particularly helpful. These days I'm more comfortable running the talk and recording my voice. I can get enough feedback from the audio to tweak the presentation. Another option is to ask someone you know and trust to watch the presentation for you. My advice is to find what works for you and then do two complete run-throughs before the presentation.

Some of us shy away from practice. We think it's better to go straight in and just do it. Mistake. If you practise you will automatically give yourself more confidence. You know what you want to say. Now you need to focus on *how* you want to say it and practise it until you can say it well under pressure.

Here are some tips to help you be your own coach – whether you watch yourself back on video or in the mirror.

- **Feet** Are they grounded? Keep them as still as you can and only move between ideas otherwise you'll distract the audience. To help, imagine your feet have roots in the ground or that you're standing in warm, yielding sand.
- **Knees** Keep them soft and not locked as that sends tension through the body.
- **Spine** It should be straight and long. Don't slump. To ensure you have an upright posture practise with a book on your head. Don't laugh, it works!

- **Shoulders** Keep them relaxed and heavy. Try to imagine you have very heavy angel wings – it will help you to drop your shoulders.
- **Arms** Use them. Imagine air under the armpits. Clamping them makes them tense. Use open and relaxed gestures.
- **Head** Keep a check on nodding. People who nod a lot lack credibility so keep it to a minimum.
- **Eye contact** Make sure you look up and out when you're speaking. When you practise put a few cushions round the room as imaginary people. Direct one line of your presentation at each person and imagine seeing them think about what you're saying. It helps on the day to imagine you're talking to one person at a time.
- **Speech** Short thoughts. Lots of full stops and emphasis.

Go – How to Feel Confident On the Day

The simplest way to do well on the day – protect your time. The old saying 'Energy flows where attention goes' sums up the true meaning of giving a good presentation. Focus your attention on the presentation like a laser. If someone else books your diary they need to know that at least a couple of hours (ideally more) before the presentation is sacrosanct.

Order the Butterflies

You may have butterflies in your stomach. All good performers do. Getting those butterflies to fly in formation is what counts on the day. When you breathe in, turn your nerves to excitement and think positively. Remind yourself this is going to be good for the audience.

Stretch

The main thing that matters physically is to get energy flowing on the day. It doesn't matter what you do as long as you stretch and move and wake up the body before you talk to an audience. If you have a long journey to get to the presentation venue, make sure you have a chance to unfurl from all the sitting before you walk out on stage.

Pilates teacher and ex-professional ballet dancer Harvey Klein explains:

The powerful essence of someone comes from not just an outer style of doing something – it actually is from within the person, breathing and moving to their full capacity. Think about a cat stretching – all the joints moving freely. Even old cats still do that stretch. We don't do that stretch. But if you can move freely, from your fingertips to your toe tips, if you can stretch properly, then you're powering up your breath, powering up your core, letting the blood flow properly. There's nothing stuck or contained. What matters is what's underneath – a deep-down core that actually helps you breathe properly, so the foundations are right. The outer body then expresses that free flow of energy.

This is not about doing an extreme gym workout, simply about doing something that gets the blood flowing, and allows you to stretch, breathe and become present to the body. Walk outside for 10 minutes or do a few stretches before you leave the house in the morning. It will give you the presence to your body and the self-knowledge so central to gravitas. See Principle 1 (see pages 23–42 for a reminder.

Countdown

The countdown to a presentation is key. Don't get stuck on email or dealing with a crisis elsewhere. Delegate ruthlessly so you can place your attention on giving your audience what they need. These are the essentials.

- Go into the room at least half an hour before to check out the set-up. Make sure your notes/slides are ready. Have everything organised so you feel safe.
- Give yourself the once-over in the mirror. You're all set.
- Go quiet inside. Feel heavy. Keep visualising how you want it to be.
- Map out your key points. Hear yourself say the first few lines in your head, slowly and calmly.
- Find somewhere quiet to sit or stand.
- Feel your spine lengthen, your shoulders drop, breathe into your back.
- Check in with your nerves – notice emotion and let it be.
- Breathe low into the fear and turn it to excitement.
- Breathe into your belly, relax your shoulders and jaw.
- Yawn and let the breath drop low and wide into your spine.
- Focus on your audience. Take a few moments to mingle with a few people from the audience. If you're feeling up to it, find out a bit about them. Being tuned into your audience this way is a great step to make the audience the hero. When you have chatted to individuals you will realise they are all just people who have come to hear you talk. It can be a good nerves neutraliser if you don't know your audience.

Ready to Go

What you do just before the presentation is crucial. People make the mistake of expelling nerves by rushing around, chatting, emailing and looking at notes. Any performer will tell you that you need to start from a place of stillness, not spin. Think of the moment before a rocket takes off, that quiet five, four, three, two, one, before the incredible power of the blast-off. Find that stillness before you launch into speech and you will find that you are able to gather up a rocket-fuelled power that engages your audiences. Here's how to manage the minutes before a presentation, whether you are in the room waiting for the audience or sitting and listening to the speaker before you.

Channel Positive Past

If you start to doubt that you can do it, go back to a positive past memory. See yourself facing a challenge in the past and succeeding. Make the movie, see it, feel it, hear it. If you could do it then you can do it now. (See Principle 7 on pages 147–162.)

Visualise Positive Future

See the audience supporting you, applauding and rooting for you. Focus on how good it will be. If your mouth goes dry take sips of water, remember to relax your feet and breathe low and wide. (A dry mouth is a sign of too much adrenalin and cortisol. Low, wide breathing will help to calm your system.)

Focus on the Present in Presentation

You're going to give your audience something that will help them. Channel a feeling of generosity. Then give the present gracefully. Be present. When you have a great present to give someone you don't thrust it at them. You check in with them. You pause, you wait. You smile. Do the same in presentation. Set an intention for your energy – how do you want to be? Then breathe, smile and relax – make it about them not you.

Get the Butterflies Flying in Formation

As you step up you want a surge of positive adrenalin. Breathe into it – breathe down into the tickly sicky feeling and breathe the butterflies into smooth formation. Let the breathing be slow and relaxed. No effort. Simply breathe out and then wait for the in-breath, relax your shoulders and allow the breath to drop into all the places that feel tense and nervous. Allow the breath to melt and soften those places so you feel the butterflies calm down and start to fly in formation – a feeling of total focus on your audience and your intention.

Rename Your Nerves

Remember, as we explored in Principle 1 (see pages 23–42) that nerves are just a feeling. Let them swirl around and call them 'being alive' or 'fun'. If it works for Bruce Springsteen it can work for you!

Do the FOFBOC

Be still, no fidgeting. Breathe low and wide into your stomach and back and relax your shoulders. Sit up tall and feel your energy gently fill the room. Feel your blood pumping and your energy tingling. Keep your feet firmly planted on the ground – the FOFBOC exercise (or dragon's tail feeling) that we looked at in Principle 1 (see page 30) and that hopefully you've been practising as you get ready for take-off. Well, now's the time to really get grounded. When I present, as I step out I want my feet to feel as comfortable and relaxed as when I'm standing in my house with people I love and trust.

> *You have to be grounded. I think it's why I find it*
> *difficult to perform in heels – my feet need to feel earthed.*
> *There is a weight in being present. You give yourself a*
> *moment and you find gravity and you become grounded.*
> *It allows your self-consciousness to disappear as you*
> *focus on your ideas and the audience.*
> INDIGO WILLIAMS, PERFORMANCE POET

Final Five Checklist

1. **Breathe** – low and wide as you step out to the front.
2. **Put the brakes on** – remember nerves speed you up, so take your time.

3. Project – your voice needs to reach the back wall.

4. Smile – see the audience as friends.

5. Be yourself – it's the true secret to gravitas.

Then, you're off! Make a graceful start, connect to the audience – a welcome and thank you usually goes down a treat – and you're up and running. Enjoy it!

Meetings

Most meetings lack gravitas. They lack impact and they lack purpose. And they definitely lack fun. Meetings are supposed to change things, to achieve action. That's the whole point of bringing everyone together. But rather than being productive most meetings are an aimless waste of time, or worse, competitive environments where people battle for status and air space.

If you want to run a successful meeting you need to create a meeting of minds – helping people to move from an environment where everyone is guarding their own little corner jealously, to a *we* environment, where people are able to be open and supportive and move towards a common purpose.

In this chapter you'll find practical tips and tricks to help you express yourself with gravitas in meetings. If you follow these tips nobody will be checking their mobile because they'll be with you all the way, listening intently. No one's going to interrupt or claim your ideas as their own because they've been paying close attention to what you're saying – they won't be able to help it! Your colleagues will choose to listen, not judge; to contribute, not compete.

If you create this kind of environment you'll gain more influence and more gravitas. That will affect the team too. Others around you will be influenced by the positivity you create.

Get Ready

Thinking ahead is the key to meetings. It's the *chronos* approach we discussed in Principle 7 (see page 150). If you can think strategically through time to make sure you are completely ready then your meetings will be effective, short and useful. When you think of the cost of everyone's time in the room, making your meetings really work seems a sensible focus.

Above all a good meeting is clear on purpose, ideally a common purpose. If everyone in the room is focused on one clear goal that needs to be achieved then the meeting is likely to get somewhere.

Is Your Meeting Entirely Necessary?

If your meeting is to be taken seriously it needs to have a purpose that is central to gravitas. So the key question is – do you actually need this meeting? Is there a specific achievable outcome that everyone in the room is involved in? If not, don't waste their time. Do you need to be face to face? If not, do it on the phone or on a video call. Generation Y will love you for it.

Another good rule of thumb for deciding whether to have a meeting is whether it's about information or emotion. If it's purely informational – an update, it can happen on the phone. But if there are ideas to explore, if you will need to read responses and tune into the emotional temperature then you need to get people together. The more people know that you only call meetings when they are really needed and that your meetings are called for a purpose, the more they will respect them.

Reconnaissance

Meeting preparation benefits from some clever detective work. If you want to influence someone think their thoughts, feel their feelings and speak their words. If you don't know enough about their feelings, thoughts and words then you need to do some research.

Dig out objections long before you get into the room. Go around and ask questions, canvas opinion – whether you talk informally to people in the days beforehand or arrange a pre-meeting. Ask intelligent questions before you get into the room. Joanna Motion is a highly experienced fundraiser and in her career has dealt with countless vice-chancellors in universities across the globe and the high-net worth individuals who support their campaigns. Her advice for challenging situations? 'I have a mantra for almost any situation: What are the issues? Who are the big players? How do we move this one forward?' Her advice is clear when it comes to reconnaissance before a meeting: 'Get to know the territory. Go round – ask what should I understand? Almost everybody responds to being asked for advice. Tune into culture and backstory before the meeting.'

Get Set

Meetings are rituals. There is *arrival, greeting, ice-breaker, core content, wrap-up* and *exit*. You need to have a sense of readiness for each stage. If the meeting is important run through how you want to be at each stage. Then you have some ideas up your sleeve, whether you use them or not.

What mood do you want to create? What are you going to wear? Where are you going to sit? These aspects of a meeting are more important than you might realise. Get them right and you boost your status and gravitas.

Arrival – Make the Right Impression

Gravitas, when it comes to making the right impressions, is also affected by your sartorial style. There are two things to consider when it comes to how you dress for a meeting. What's the style of the organisation? What makes you feel comfortable? You need to be able to forget what you're wearing so you can focus in the meeting. It's why gravitas in style is often brilliantly cut, pared down and minimal. A style that makes you look really pulled together without taking hours every morning.

If you're meeting new people getting the right style can also be a matter of reconnaissance. If you can look like you fit in style-wise it's much easier to make a connection. If you need to check in with the style of the organisation you can find out a lot on the Internet. What are people wearing in the company photos or videos? Or talk to someone who works there. I've even heard of people going to sit in a cafe near the organisation to watch people coming in and out.

If the meeting matters, it will certainly help you to look the part.

Greeting – Shake Hands Well

A handshake is key to gravitas because it tells someone a great deal about how calm and confident you are. Below are some tips. Practise them socially so you get the hang of them before you need them in high-stakes work situations. They will work best for you when they are on autopilot so you can focus on the other person.

Because the contact with your hand communicates information about the rest of you it's crucial to be calm and composed before the meeting. Get there with some time to spare so you aren't rushing in. Make sure you aren't overladen with bags and papers so the handshake can be graceful. Make sure you are standing.

When you shake hands remember that gravitas is about the balance of forces. You need to give them a sense of calm, grounded energy as you shake hands. It's a short moment but it tells them a huge amount about you. Avoid the politician's trick of a palm-down handshake to assert authority. Gravitas is far too self-assured to need to play power games like that. See the person as an equal and offer an open palm with the thumb at the top. It sounds strange but as you shake hands consciously relax your breathing. It affects the nervous system and feeds into a relaxed handshake.

You want 50 per cent awareness of your own calm state. Think status (see Principle 2 on page 45). Stand tall and keep your head still to boost your authority. But that status must also be balanced and connected. (If it's not, breathe low and wide and relax your shoulders. It may help to go back to Principle 1 and remind yourself of the FOFBOC exercise and the Dragon's Tail, see pages 30–31.) Being physically grounded and relaxed communicates in your handshake because, to paraphrase the song, the arm bone's connected to the spine, the spine's connected to the pelvis, the pelvis is connected to the legs, etc. You get the picture.

Ice-breaker

As people come in, make time to connect individually and tune into their mood. You want 50 per cent awareness and real, genuine interest in them. Think connection (see Principle 2 on page 45). You need genuine warmth and kindness to balance your authority. This is so key to the gravitas of a great first impression. Smile as if the person is an old friend you haven't seen for ages – we like people who are genuinely pleased to see us. It lifts the mood because if they have any social awareness they smile back at you and everyone feels good.

At this point you can tune into the energy and mood of the people in the room. If you've done some reconnaissance you'll know if there are hidden agendas or fears. If you see levels of stress or anxiety that you hadn't anticipated, check in with people. Let them get rid of emotional baggage if, say, they've had to rush because the train was late or a child is ill. When you know the context you can accommodate them. Let them leave early or keep their phone on. This allows people to feel understood, which is key to the empathy of gravitas, and it allows them to focus.

Then there's the moment where you are invited to sit, or if it's your meeting, you do the inviting. The key is to have a sense of quiet grace and presence. Take it slowly. No rushing. This is the moment to really ground yourself and pay attention. You need to be present – in *kairos* (see Principle 7 on page 150). Move with conscious awareness and sit down gracefully. Make others feel at ease with you.

Sit Strategically

Choose your chair wisely. The power seat is usually facing the door with the window behind you. If you don't need to be in charge but want influence it can help to sit on the right-hand side of the power person. If you want to avoid confrontation with someone sit on the corner or to their side, don't sit opposite them.

Go

The moment when the meeting starts is when you need to set a common *intention* and then pay *attention* so you can steer your colleagues to a good result (as we explored in Principle 7 on page 150).

Respect Time

If you're chairing be in control of the timing. You need to be able to keep people to time so that they don't lose focus. Here's how:

Frame the timing from the start. Say that you will make sure the meeting finishes on time right from the off. If time is tight it can help to have an allotted time for each agenda item. If you have to move the agenda on remind people that you want to stick to the timings so that they can get out on time. After all, no one will mind if you finish early.

If you know you have a tendency to get lost in the moment – you are a *kairos* rather than *chronos* type (see Principle 7 on page 150) – then nominate someone in the room to keep you to time. I am very *kairos* as a speaker and I love this strategy. It keeps me to time and *chronos* people hugely appreciate that.

Be vigilant to airtime huggers. If you see someone trying to monopolise the meeting gently but firmly move the agenda on. Encourage quieter members to air their views, but don't force it. Let everyone speak and give them equal time to do so. This irons out cultural differences in how people speak up and how much they feel they should speak. Even conversation hoggers sometimes do it because they fear silences. Take that fear away.

Core Content – Find the Common Purpose

When it comes to meetings, 'The key problem' said Eleanor Roosevelt, 'is to find some binding interest to make them feel part of the whole, and to stimulate each one to make [their] particular contribution.'[1] One simple maxim – journalist Gavin Esler's creation can help you with this: 'Who am I? Who are we? What's the common purpose?'[2]

Purpose, as we've discovered, is key to planning meetings with gravitas. Finding a genuine common purpose is also key to delivering them. The people in the room with you need to fully buy into that purpose. Then you create a we in the room.

One good way to do this is to celebrate and appreciate what's already working. It creates a positivity and energy that feeds the rest of the meeting. Don't be so focused on the goal that you fail to celebrate what you've already achieved.

Remember to state the common purpose upfront. You may think that people know why they're there, but in our busy lives sometimes we need to be reminded and re-inspired. In particular, re-engage them with the vision – what success will look like. Or, if they're more risk-averse, what they need to avoid.

See The Bigger Picture

When you have a clear common purpose it's about stepping back and seeing the bigger picture so that you can help bridge between the different perspectives of people in the room. Essentially it's about being able to flex your empathy and objectivity muscles. See Principle 6 for advice on being a leveller (see page 131). Levellers lead great meetings because they are self-aware and able to manage challenges without letting it make them anxious or defensive. When you stay in control you are better able to steer the emotions of the group positively.

Join the Dots

Be the person who joins up the dots rather than is the dots. Turn the light on other people there quite rapidly. Understand the context in which you're operating. Research that and pay attention. Take your signals from the other people. Tune into other people's anxieties and motivations – those are the skills that enable you to deliver and reach a point of mutual respect. Doff your cap to what they do and admire it and then win understanding for your track record – demonstrate your confidence, competence. I'm contributing in my way and I value and am impressed by what you do.

JOANNA MOTION, UNIVERSITY FUNDRAISER AND SPEAKER

Name the Worries

You've dealt with any anxiety that people brought into the room with them, but what happens if the content of the meeting itself makes people tense up and shift in their seats? Face up to it and move the energy on. It's a lot about helping people be aware of their collective responsibility to the mood. But you have to go first.

If you want a positive mood and it's not there, take responsibility for creating a different energy. If there is negativity in the room, what's it about? What's the unspoken fear? If you are in a senior position, can you name and frame the problems positively? For example, 'I know that we're all really feeling the big pressure of the project, and it's great that we're on track for a good result.' Sometimes naming the fact that people are feeling, say, pressure, and giving them a positive frame on it, allows people to come out of their worries for a moment and to pay attention to the room. Be careful not to judge. Accept what people are feeling. Put a positive frame on it and move on.

The Power of Good Listening
(Or Don't Speak Unless You Improve the Silence)

Remember not only to say the right thing in the right place, but far more difficult still, leave unsaid the wrong thing at the tempting moment.

BENJAMIN FRANKLIN, PRESIDENT OF USA

Your job, if you want gravitas, is to ensure that everyone feels acknowledged and heard. Even if you're not chairing, you can do this for people who might be feeling marginalised by listening fully to everyone when they speak and acknowledging the contributions of others.

Just as there are three kinds of empathy (see Principle 6 on page 135) there are three kinds of listening. When you listen in a meeting, choose your gear:

- Are you **listening reflectively** to gather information?
- Are you **listening supportively** to build and coach others?
- Are you **listening for possibility** to look for ways forward?

If you know how you are listening you will be clearer on how to respond. If you are *reflecting*, join the dots for the audience, help them find common ground and identify challenges. If you are in *supportive* listening, ask lots of questions when you speak and feed back what is working. And if you are listening *for possibility*, speak when you need to comment on something that will move you towards a goal. I have a client who knows to speak only when decisions in meetings are likely to move the share price of the company she represents either up or down.

Ultimately the quality of what you say reflects the quality of your listening. All good listeners were good speakers first. Before you speak do a quick check-in with yourself. Is what you're about to say coming from listen-to-me ego? The grown-up equivalent of the schoolchild waving their hand at the teacher – 'Me, me, me!'

Or is it coming from your better half, the part of you that contributes to the group? The ego self usually has little to offer the group while the higher self usually offers something of value. Know the difference. Listen to the whole room and the dynamic currents of the discussion. Does what you have to say add something to it? If it does, speak.

Speak Up

If meetings make you nervous, remember that they are about contributing not competing. Think of how you can serve rather than whether your ideas are impressive. The antidote to creeping dread – the fear of speaking up in a meeting – is to be a better listener. Worrying about whether what you say is good enough is too much about you. Get over it. Listen positively not competitively. Know when to speak and when to be silent (and make sure you do both).

When you're ready to speak, scribble down three bullet points and jump in. Don't overthink it. Say it loud and say it clear. Demand gracefully in your energy and your clarity of purpose that you be heard.

Avoid ums, ers and qualifiers – 'I think', 'I'm not sure if' – they weaken your impact and your gravitas. Levellers say it straight. If someone says something useful give credit where it's due. It's also a great way to get your voice into the room in a positive way. Give genuine appreciation – it must be honest, succinct and concrete.

The Power of Questions

When you're really listening you'll know what questions to ask. The better your questions, the better others think. Here are some examples:

To open a discussion
- What do we think about this?
- What do we know?
- What does this mean for us?

To clarify existing beliefs, to challenge assumptions, to take an audience into a different way of thinking, to open minds
- Is there a different viewpoint?
- What are we assuming here?
- If we didn't assume this, what would be different?

To dig deeper
- What's the evidence to support this?
- What's the underlying intention here?
- What's the cause?

To explore consequences
- What would happen if?
- Why is this important?
- What questions do we need to ask about this?

Wrap Up

How you wrap up is important. Learn from music. Go back to the original theme of the meeting and reprise it. Remind the audience of the purpose. Acknowledge the great contributions that have been made and the distance you've travelled. Set action points that everyone can agree to and commit to achieving. Without this commitment there's no point to a meeting.

Exit

Exit gracefully and acknowledge people as they leave. If you notice that anyone looks worried and needs further support, spend a little time with them if you can. Make sure that an email is sent out to thank everyone for their time and gracefully remind them of the actions they committed to.

Telephone Calls and Teleconferences

Finding a way to speak with gravitas and impact on the phone is vital in a connected world. As our working lives span the globe sometimes a phone line is your main tool for making personal contact.

Phone calls, whether you're talking to one person or a hundred, can feel really tricky. You can't see the person; the person can't see you. All you have to go on is words, pace, energy and voice tone. It's even harder with teleconferences because you might have a number of people in different time zones, with different first languages, many of whom you've never met in person. It can feel impossible. Who speaks first? How can you tell if you're giving the audience what they need? There's no appreciative smiles to tell you you're doing well nor dead eyes or bored looks to tell you they've lost you.

Learn from radio presenter Peter Everett (see box, overleaf). Seeing a person opposite you can transform your delivery. Even if you're on your own you can stick a photo of someone you love on your computer screen. Luckily radio has many more good tips for phone calls. Radio is the medium that feels like a hug. There's an intimacy and a conversational warmth we can all learn from when it comes to making our calls better. In particular, what will help you is smiling and gesture. Read on to found out how:

Use Your Normal Voice

One of the deadly sins of the telephone is using a phone voice. This is the same problem that happens to some radio presenters when they talk into a microphone. The radio producer Peter Everett explains how it happens and what you can do about it.

It's a very unnatural thing, to talk into a microphone. People sometimes become stilted. It can become best-man-at-a-wedding syndrome if they're not very experienced. To help people with that, rather than be on the other side of the glass with the engineer I'll actually go into the studio and sit at the table with them, and get some eye contact going so that they're talking to a human being.

Use your normal voice. Most of the time when I hear people talking on the radio I think, 'Why don't you talk in your normal voice?' The worst thing is to be 'plonking' (that local radio newsreader formulaic sing-song where you deliver the words of a sentence, like putting down stones in a line). It's overemphatic. The 'if I just do a rise and fall at regular intervals I'll get away with it'. As a listener, I think, 'Just get on with it, tell me in a normal voice.'

You can easily get away from that. If you are really engaged with what you're talking about, you will automatically hit the right words. Speak in a way that implies, 'I find this very interesting and I am highly engaged by it and I think that you will find it interesting as well.' Communicate excitement, interest, engagement with what you're saying.

Get Ready

The first thing to do when preparing for important phone calls is to think about how you come across. You want a voice that is full of the relaxed warmth and poise of gravitas. And there's a very good secret from radio to help you do just that.

The Radio Voice Secret

She spoke seldom but when she did
it was in a voice like dark brown velvet.
JOSEPHINE TEY, *MISS PYM DISPOSES*

The biggest lesson I have learnt from working with seasoned radio presenters? The power of the *dark brown voice*. If you're wondering what on earth that is it's the old expression for the relaxed warmth that you hear in the great radio presenters' voices. You know those voices – they make you feel like you're having a fireside chat with the presenter even though you can't see their face.

So, how do you do *dark brown voice*? Smile. Watch a good radio presenter about to go on air and you'll see them, just before they go live, consciously light up their face with a smile, as if someone they care about is sitting opposite them in the studio.

And it's not just any old smile. It has to be genuine. We can hear whether a smile is real or fake – even without seeing the person. In fact, recent research by Dr Amy Drahota, research fellow at the School of Health Sciences and Social Work, University of Portsmouth, showed that we can hear three types of smile: a broad grin (the Duchenne smile), a half smile and the smile we do when we're trying to suppress a laugh.[1]

Researchers found that the smile that was easiest to hear was the broad grin, the natural smile we do with those we like, which crinkles up our eyes. It warms the voice by allowing the body and breath to relax and gives it the resonant, friendly brown-voice quality.

Smiling also adds melody to the voice. John J. Ohala, at the University of California, Berkeley has suggested that the smile evolved as a tool to signal approachability in sound. When you smile it changes the acoustics in your mouth and picks up a higher frequency in the vocal tract so it sounds higher.[2]

The veteran broadcaster Angela Rippon once gave me a great tip. She told me that the art to good broadcasting is to imagine you are speaking to one person that you love. It was the tip her father gave her when she took up her first job as a news-anchor at the BBC. Try it – you'll hear a big difference in your voice. Test it using a voice recorder.

1. Record yourself saying something in your normal style: the days of the week is a good start.
2. Now record the same words again, this time with your brown voice and a smile (it can help to imagine that you are talking to a great friend).
3. Now listen to the two recordings. You will really notice a difference between the flatness of your phone voice when you're talking to thin air and without a smile, and the lovely, natural warmth and music of your brown voice when you're imagining talking to a person you love. This one simple act will transform calls and radio interviews.

Gesture Matters

The biggest misconception about phone calls is that the body doesn't matter and that the normal rules of speaking and gesturing can go by the wayside. Not true. Good voice-over artists will tell you to go against this instinct because what they understand is that it's the iconic gestures that boost your voice tone. It's why you see them in sound booths in recording studios standing up and using lots of gestures. It orchestrates the vocal expression beautifully. Simply – you *hear gesture* in the voice. You should gesture even more when an audience can't see you to get increased vocal energy. Test it on a voice recorder and you'll really hear a difference.

Get Set

The call's in the diary. Now, to make it worthwhile you need to ensure you present your thinking in a way that earns your listeners' attention. The truth is that most audiences on the phone are easily distracted. They are tempted to check their email and then there's the world of social media. It's crucial that you get their attention otherwise the call will be a waste of time.

If you don't know much about the person you're speaking to, go back to the Presentation and Talks chapter and look at the realist questions (see page 171). Take time to walk a mile in their shoes. Having done this it's time to think about creating concise content that will engage them.

Keep it Punchy

What matters above all on the phone is concise punchy content. Face the fact that if it's a teleconference most people are checking their email while listening to you. You need to take the news-editor rule and 'Talk to the clever 14-year-old'. Unless you keep it clear and bite-sized their email will win and you will lose. One way to keep their attention (an old teachers' trick) is to let people know you will be asking questions and involving them. Then they have to stay with you. Subtle pauses also make people focus their attention. Use them.

While you don't need a word-for-word breakdown of what you want to say it is helpful to have a loose script or plan. You can divert from this if needed, but it serves to give the calls a shape and structure. Go back to the Headlines, Main Story, Wrap exercise in Principle 3 (see page 72) and look at Presentations and Talks (see pages 167–186) as they will help you distil your ideas down in a way that makes them impactful for your listeners.

Articulate

If people are straining to listen, they're unlikely to take in much of what you say so make sure you articulate. Don't let the words trickle down the drain. You must give your sentences energy. This keeps vitality in the call and makes you sound more credible.

Focus on the ends of words – those final consonants are essential to meaning.

On the phone you can really articulate, especially if your audience doesn't speak English as their first language.

If you have a quiet moment before the call, do a quick articulation warm-up (see Principle 4 on pages 85–104 for more on voice and speech). You need to be alone to do this so find any empty office or meeting room. And if you can do it in front of a mirror, all the better.

1. Speak the days of the week or count to 10. Really get your mouth moving.
2. Then do a big yawn and speak as you yawn to stretch everything out.
3. Then say the days of the week again. Exaggerate all the vowel sounds.
4. Say the days of the week one last time. Exaggerate all the consonants.
5. Now when you speak it should feel more 'muscular', to borrow an acting term. As if everything is warmed up.

Generate a Positive Feeling

Now generate a good feeling about the call. You might remember a nice phone call in the past or visualise the call going well in the future.

Go

Phone calls can be surprisingly anxiety-inducing, especially when they are important professionally. The tips that follow will allow you to exude calm, confident gravitas when you speak on the phone.

Be Pleased to Hear Them

If a call is booked in the diary, a nice touch is to answer the phone normally. When you hear the person's name smile broadly. The person will 'hear' the smile and it will make them feel welcomed and positive.

Picture Your Audience

One way to make yourself feel more settled is to picture your audience sitting in their offices listening to you talk. Imagine them finding the call useful and see them looking interested. Keep asking yourself what they need from you, what's in it for them. Newscasters say 'So what?' In other words, how is what you've got to say relevant to them?

Stand Up

If you want authority and gravitas in your voice on the phone, stand up. It doubles your authority instantly. If you are sitting down and things gets tricky, again assert your authority by standing up.

Start Well

Starting with a story, a statistic or positive feedback works well. Research shows that the beginning and the end of a call are the parts that most people remember, so start with a good feeling. Saying something about yourself, the group and your common purpose makes a good opening too. Get them inspired early on. Without body language to read it's vital that you get feedback from everyone involved in the call. Make sure you schedule this into the agenda.

Stay Focused

You must keep your listening sharp. Even on the phone people know if you are distracted because your responses are slightly behind. It will irritate them. If you need to really listen try either closing your eyes or writing notes – whichever focuses you better. If you need an empathetic connection then the closed eyes will help as you will really be emotionally present. If you need to be more intellectually supportive and solutions focused then writing notes may help you to think more strategically.

Be Expressive

Match your voice to your goal and the needs of the audience. Think of the four voices in Principle 2 – king/queen and warrior, carer and creator (see page 50). Play between them depending on the mood you want to create. Stand up if you can. It gives your voice energy. Keep using gestures to keep your voice moving. Vary the tone of your voice. Let each phrase and idea have a different energy to keep it interesting. Focus and really listen. Don't be tempted to check texts and emails just because they can't see you.

Wrap Well

At the end of the conversation create positivity among the group. Finish on time, or earlier, with plenty of energy. Smile as you finish and punch out the last word that you say. Don't tail off. Sum up and follow up with what happens next. Keep it short and sweet. Did you ever hear anyone complain that a call was too short? Plan the close. Warn everyone you are coming to a close. Summarise the key points and give a call to action. Make sure everyone knows the next steps.

Above all, enjoy your phone calls. And remember, listen, listen, listen to the radio. If you want to know what works for a good call radio has most of the answers. Listen to it and practise. Calls are an art form that can be perfected with practice.

Interviews and Pitches

Got an interview coming up? An important idea to pitch? You want to get information over to the other person. You want to give them a true idea of who you really are or what your proposal can offer. You want to be yourself – only better. With gravitas. With impact. You at your distilled, authoritative best.

That's what this section is all about – how to create the best impression in those scary interviews and pitches. What matters most in these situations is getting the balance right between your gravitas and warmth. You want to be taken *seriously* and you also want to be *warm* and *conversational*. They want to see that your words and actions match, that you are congruent, trustworthy.

Why? Because they're going to need and *want* to see you again. This combination of authoritative ease, warmth and credibility is powerful. We looked at it in Principle 3 (see pages 63–83). This chapter is about testing it for real in the situations where getting it right can make a *big* difference to your life.

Getting interviews and pitches spot on involves a whole skill set of psychological and physical strategies combined with performance tactics that ensure you create the right impression. You can learn to do all this by becoming your own coach and breaking your preparation down into small tasks so that you can fit it in around the other demands of daily life.

Get Ready – How to Prepare

Gravitas in an interview or pitch situation is about being relaxed and natural so that you can have a great conversation between like minds.

Research Ritual

The more you know about the person or people you're going to meet, the better. Some clever research is a great way to spark your curiosity and interest. With so much information available on the Internet you can build up a picture in no time. Find out who's going to be interviewing you. If you can find any audio or video of them, even better. That way you get a sense of them being a real living, breathing person.
Look out for:

- **How you are similar.** Find things you have in common. We like people like us and we like finding things in common. What's your common ground? What's your common purpose? What do you have that they need? What fear or problem do you have the answer to?
- **Their style.** How do they look and what does that tell you about them? This might influence the way you dress on the day or even the way you choose to present yourself.
- **Their speech.** Notice their voice tone and the words they use. Are they formal or informal? Fast or slow? Do they come across as long-winded and verbose or concise and succinct?
- **Their attitude.** Are they enthusiastic or thoughtful, introvert or extrovert? Are they serious or do they smile a lot?
- **What they say.** Do they talk about what they want or what they want to avoid? Listen out for the words they use about themselves and what others say about them too.
- **Their profile.** Do they write a blog or have a website? What does it say about them? Have they been interviewed in the press?

- **Their preferences.** What do they love? What do they hate? What's important to them? Can you find out whom they admire and what they fear?

You're not trying to be a carbon copy. It's about tuning in to the things that inspire you when you read about them and zoning in on the parallels between you. If you discover that their style is wildly different to yours, don't go all out to try to be like them.

Gravitas is about the match between the inner world and your outer expression. Don't try to be something you're not.

'I Have a Dream' – See Success

Research has shown that in interviews panels are far more influenced by your vision of the future than your track record, however impressive it may be. When Martin Luther King said 'I have a dream' he could see it. Walt Disney used to talk about the future as 'big and glittering'.[1] To access similar levels of inspired gravitas in yourself you need to inspire yourself with the vision of what it will look like to get the job or win the pitch. You have to see yourself getting through. This is a psychological must. You need to know what getting the job or winning the pitch will be like because they see it in your eyes, even if they don't consciously know what makes you stand out. When they ask you questions and when they grill you on your skills, talents, aims and ideas they can actually *see you seeing* something powerful.

Questions, Questions

What are they going to ask? Will you have the answers? Will they trick you? What if you go blank? The scary part about interviews and pitches is the uncertainty. The trick is to get inside their heads and think up all the possible questions they might ask.

1. Imagine looking over at yourself from the other side of the table as if you're the one doing the interviewing.

2. Imagine the interviewer's fear of getting it wrong. Think about what they're going to need to know to be sure you're the right person. If you were the interviewer what would you be curious about? What would you need to know? What's already sparked your interest on the CV or pre-pitch information?

3. Get a sheet of paper and write down questions. The good and the bad. Those you dream of and those you dread. The ones you know they're bound to ask. The ones that in previous pitches and interviews would have given you goosebumps and resulted in you mumbling.

4. There's one question left isn't there? You're right. The last question. It's the worst thing ever. Write down the ugly question, the one you dread ever coming up. Face it now and face it down.

Mastermind the Answers

Then there are the answers. The main challenge here is that you obviously know way more about your life than your interviewer ever needs to. So don't shift into information overload. It's useful to think yourself into the mind of a chat-show host. Handpick the most powerful stories. The most memorable ones. Then get them clear and concise so they are sitting ready for you if you need them.

Keep your answers simple and succinct. If the interviewers need more information they will ask for it. Say only what is essential and then zip it.

Having a simple structure to your answers works wonders:

1. **Point** – the key idea you want to communicate.

2. **Reference** – connect that point to a concrete example. Show specific credibility.

3. **Comment** – make that point unique to you and give the interviewer a sense of how it will be beneficial. Your purpose.

Make sure your answers are punchy:

- Drill down to specific facts, figures and stories. Don't generalise.
- Make your stories real – populate them with real people, places and events.
- If you're talking about your skills make sure you give a specific example of how you used them.
- Keep a stock of stories that you can apply to any questions. Of course there's always a chance you'll be asked something that's a complete surprise, but if you have a toolkit of information ready you can usually pull something together in the moment.

Get Set – Perfect Practice

Once you've got your head together psychologically it's time to think about how to practise to get your mind, voice and body working in perfect harmony. You want your whole self to be working like a well-oiled machine so that there are no rough edges or gritty hindrances to ruin the day.

Practising makes *all* the difference to gravitas under pressure. No performer ever goes on stage without having rehearsed. No sportsperson walks on to a field without hours and hours of training. Perfectionists among you – a word of warning! Be careful because you can be too rehearsed and polished. You want to avoid learning things word for word. You want to be organised but not overscripted – that looks fake. Practise in a loose way. Don't fix everything. Practice is more about honing your awareness so that you know how you come across under pressure.

When you're asked a question, and once you have an answer:

- Give the headlines of it – **Point**
- Give the core content – **Reference**
- Summarise – **Comment**

Sit Up

Your posture must be as crisp as your delivery:

- Sit up and back with a straight spine, keeping your tailbone to the back of the chair.
- Project your voice to the back of the room with relaxed energy.
- Make your words work for you. Speak them clearly and with commitment.

Set out your stall: How to use sign posts

When you answer a question, pause, then say something like 'Two points. First …' It has the great benefit of stopping someone interrupting you, keeping the questioner at bay. It makes people listen because they are thinking 'I wonder what number two is?' They've told you what they're going to say and you'd better sit back and let them finish their piece. You would feel rude as the interviewer if you didn't allow them to get through their two points. You've set out your stall, 'This is what I want to say, be kind enough to allow me to say it.'

SIMON JACK, BUSINESS AND ECONOMICS PRESENTER,

TODAY, BBC RADIO 4

So, how do you find your brakes? Simple. Say what you've got to say then *close your mouth*. It's incredibly effective.

1. Stand in front of a mirror.
2. Say your name and then watch your mouth close.
3. Breathe through your nose and relax your eyes.

If you've practised the above exercise what you'll find in an interview is that you speak a number of short, focused phrases, neatly answering the question (go back to Winston Churchill in Principle 3 for more on this – see page 75). Then you close your mouth. You pause and an in-breath arrives to replace the out-breath you just spoke on (see Principle 4 on page 95). The pause gives the control back. Make it relaxed and pregnant with your focus, presence and thought. It's the interviewer's job to fill it. The pause is where the interviewer thinks about what you've said. It's where they say to themselves, 'Yes, that's interesting.'

Clear Your Diary

It's easy to treat an interview or pitch as just another date in your diary but it's wise to allow yourself a quiet lead-in to the day.

- Don't cram your diary. Keep the days before as clear as possible so that you can focus.
- You want your focus on the interview to be like a candle in the dark. Everything else must be secondary for now. That means: keeping your phone off as much as possible; putting your out-of-office message on your email; giving yourself a lengthy period of calm before you leave the house – perhaps do some stretches, a little yoga, sing to yourself in the shower or go for a short walk, or just sit quietly and visualise yourself doing the interview well.

Keep Things in Perspective

Gravitas requires an ability to keep things in perspective, to be the cool, calm pilot of the plane even when turbulence hits.

Pay real attention to how you're currently feeling about the interview or pitch. If you're like most people you're probably feeling that it is a great big looming threat. That's mainly because things that feel threatening tend to be bigger than us, close to us and happening when it's dark. If you change the way you perceive the interview or pitch you'll start to feel more positive. Remember that you're in control of your inner experience. Try this exercise:

1. Imagine the interview is on a little mobile phone screen.
2. Push the screen away from you until it's tiny and manageable.
3. Step back from it so you gain some perspective or make the screen light not dark.

After doing this exercise you'll find that your concerns seem smaller, lighter and more manageable – a molehill rather than a mountain.

Just Before You Go Through the Door

A very good piece of advice for making a good impression – with gravitas – is to be responsible for the energy you take into the room. Set your intention. What do you dream of happening in the room? Take that energy in with you.

Open up. When we get stressed we see a very narrow field of vision. It's good to give yourself more of a 360-degree view. Opening up is like throwing open the windows on a humid day. It releases tension.

Say something positive to yourself – your inner coach reminding you that you can do this.

Use an emotion memory to help you through. It could be:

- A place where you feel relaxed.
- A person who makes you smile.
- Something you do that makes you relaxed and happy.
- A compliment you've received to boost your confidence.
- The voice of someone who supports you.

Remember to breathe low and wide, ground your feet and be fascinated – think how you can help.

If you feel a rictus freeze your face, imagine smiling at someone you know, like and respect. This helps release tension and will encourage your interviewer to relax too.

Go

Good interviews and pitches are essentially great conversations. You need to be in a state of mind where you are prepped enough that you can walk in and be yourself. I'm very much of the belief that, as long as you are on good form, if it's right for you it will go your way. The tips that follow are designed to help you relax, trust yourself and find your voice. Trusting your ethos (see page 11) and Principle 7, on responding resourcefully (see page 157) will also support you in this.

Tune In

When you walk in, tune in. Stop. Take a moment. Breathe and connect with your interviewer's energy and match it. Don't bounce in like a puppy if they are cool cats. Or vice versa, if you sense enthusiasm, up your energy. You want peripheral vision, a sense of being able to see all around you, even to the extent of awareness behind you in your back ('Eyes in the back of your head' as your mum put it). It's a relaxed presence and alertness, very different to the narrow vision we have when we are on high alert.

Listen

The absolute most important thing you must do in an interview is be really fascinated by the panel. If you are going to be able to work with them there needs to be common ground. A really great starting place for fascination is to properly listen and pay attention. Engage head, heart and gut. This creates a positive channel of communication that makes you memorable.

Really, really, really listen. The kind of listening that you do when you are genuinely interested. Not faking it. You don't have to overdo it. Show the listening in the focus in your eyes and your presence to them. That's enough. In general avoid too much nodding or eyebrow raising and uh-humming. It's like a date – don't try too hard to be liked. Be really interested in the job and what you can do for them with the confidence they'd be lucky to have you. Especially when going for senior roles. (See more on this in Principle 2 on pages 43–61).

Think Before You Speak

People who come across as knowledgeable, authoritative and thoughtful clearly listen to the question. It is evident in the way they animate their face. They're actually listening, they're not waiting to get their first point in. All of them pause.

Display the fact that you're thinking rather than being wound up like a key. It confers authority.

SIMON JACK, BUSINESS AND ECONOMICS PRESENTER,

TODAY, BBC RADIO 4

Turn Your Camera Out

The difficulty with interviews and pitches is that you can end up doing fake listening, when you're actually talking to yourself in your head. Real listening makes things quiet inside your head because you're paying full attention to the person you are talking to. If you struggle to really listen when you're nervous because your inner voice is rabbiting on, then ration it.

Have 80 per cent attention out there on the room and 20 per cent attention in your head. Be quiet inside. If internal chatter comes, remember it's only graffiti. Don't interpret any meaning from it. Instead divert attention to your body and notice your audience. Respond to them rather than any anxiety about what you think they might be thinking.

On your pauses pay attention inside your head. It may mean your eyes go a little dull, but that's fine. It means the interviewer knows you're thinking about something. Then work out what you're going to say and go for it. From then on in when you're talking your focus must be *outwards*. When you're giving attention to the world your eyes must be *alive*. Really pay attention to the other person and notice them completely.

Take Your Time

When people rush it's as if they can't wait to get it over with. The audience are thinking 'well you clearly haven't got much to say'. As the listener you write off their contribution, because you think they're gabbling their way through it.

SIMON JACK, BUSINESS AND ECONOMICS PRESENTER,

TODAY, BBC RADIO 4

Don't forget – they'd be lucky to have you! Own your ethos and trust that if it's right – and there's chemistry – it will go your way.

On Camera

The TV camera loves gravitas – and it loves passion. It's why the holy grail for newscasters, as discussed in Principle 2, is credible passion.

When you're invited on TV you really need to draw on credible passion as it will allow you to be authentic and make an impact.

Get Ready

Preparing to speak to camera is about getting right down to the essence of who you are and what you want to say so you can be clear, concise and full of credible passion. The camera loves people who are fully themselves and at ease, yet absolutely distilled. The art is to find that balance.

Trust Yourself and What You Have to Offer

You will have been invited to speak – whether it's on the company video or national news – because you know something of interest. It's really important to trust that. You are neither arrogant nor humble, but neatly in the middle. Remind yourself you're good at what you do and draw your confidence from that. Let the anchor or the reporter worry about the other side of things.

Find Your Essence and Turn Up the Dial

*What matters is having a genuine interest and passion for
your subject. TV is performance, but it's not an actor's
performance. It has to be a natural one. Yourself but turning
the volume up. And what's crucial is to be on top of the content.
Pace matters. You don't want people to be supersonic speed-wise,
because speaking too quickly is a sign of nervousness and is a
problem in TV. But if you're pausing for the information this can
be attractive and can show a degree of thought. The key thing for
a viewer is to feel confident that the person you're watching knows
what they're talking about and they are in control. Another thing
you look for is a way with words. A good vocabulary. A sense of
humour. All of those things. If you can combine your expertise
with a nice turn of phrase, a good simile, a nice metaphor,
an engaging way of putting something. It's not just
the content but the words you use to deliver it.*

GABY HORNSBY, BBC TV DOCUMENTARY DIRECTOR AND PRODUCER

How to Prep Your Content

A message map, as detailed in the Presentation and Talks chapter on page 173, is great for prepping TV content, but you need to be ultra-concise. There's another benefit to being concise – you can go notes-free. I'm pretty hardline about being on camera. Whether you're in the national news studio, on video for your company website or on a video-conference, if you're in front of a camera you need to be notes-free. Glancing down at a piece of paper is simply no good for gravitas. Go back to the Memory House exercise in Principle 3 on page 82 if you think your ability to learn lines needs support.

TV Rules of Thumb

These rules will help you prepare the right kind of content:

- **Be concise** No answer should ever be longer than a minute. A minute is a *long* time in TV. 30 seconds is ideal.
- **Prepare your answers** For each question you will be asked, have two key ideas and one as backup. Write these down as notes even if on the day you probably won't have them with you.
- **Use specifics** You need your audience to pay attention. Don't bore them with generic answers. Give them something you've thought about, something that gives your unique perspective. For each point refer to something real – something you can do, something you did or something you learnt.
- **Be credible** Give facts and figures – they give credibility and detail. Make it vivid to make it memorable.
- **Be emotional** We feel before we think, so connect to what's important to you. Talk about that – it's the best way to fire the interviewer up. You need your interviewers to care. Talk about values that matter to you and to them. Make sure you connect to their experience. Use phrases like 'Have you ever?' and 'You know when …' Talk about the emotions you felt and feel them in the moment.
- **Tell stories** Your content needs to be juicy and unique. Something they'll remember. Have neat pithy examples of all the points you want to cover. People and dramatic stories are interesting as they engage our hearts and minds. Go back to Principle 5 on pages 105–120 for more on this.

Get Set

The Power of Story

*You realise that you get more traction with your audience
if you tell a story rather than a bunch of facts. And you're
prepared to give it emphasis and conviction at the appropriate
moments. That makes people sit up and listen. This person
is telling me something I need to know.*

SIMON JACK, BUSINESS AND ECONOMICS PRESENTER,

TODAY, BBC RADIO 4

Though it is crucial to prepare, it is a fine balance. Learning your words until your eyes glaze over in the act of remembering them is a no-no. Conversational and chatty is what you're looking for. Go for bullet points and practise until you have the links clear. (Go back to Principle 3 on pages 63–83 if you need more on this.)

Think on your Feet

*Authority on air is about thought, rather than learning the words
verbatim. A lot of people learn what they want to say to the
camera, and it comes out in a sort of automated fashion.
It's much better to think your way through what you're saying,
even if it's not exactly the same form of words every time.*

JON SNOW, JOURNALIST AND PRESENTER

Go

The moment when you get in front of the camera is the moment you need to turn your lights on. Cameras require you at your most sparkly in the eyes, poised, enthusiastic and relaxed in mood. Here's how:

On-air Sparkle

The TV camera picks up light and warmth. The trick is to be your natural, sparkliest self with the dial turned up on both credibility and compassion. You also need to be concise and clear-thinking under the adrenalin rush of a studio or staring down the barrel of a camera, and once you've done the preparation, that's about calm. When you get into a studio your nerves can vanish. Seasoned broadcasters will tell you it helps to imagine you will only be on air for a short time then you can keep your energy up.

When it comes to shining on camera, the GRAVITAS acronym is designed to help you remember what to do.

G rooming On TV, hair and make-up makes all the difference. Since the footage is likely to be there for posterity, put the effort in. Looking groomed and tidy is key. If you can have it done professionally ladies, please do – a free session at the make-up counter is usually enough. Men, you too – a bit of powder hides the shine. Ask a make-up expert (at home?!) to help. The main thing to know about clothing is avoid black and white and too much pattern. Cameras can't cope with it. Primary colours are what the camera loves above all.

R elax The adrenalin of a camera will speed you up so try to keep calm. Think of the FOFBOC exercise (see page 30). Keep your breathing steady and your mind quiet. This means prepping carefully. Too much thinking makes you blink a lot and your eyes move all over the place. Better to be prepped, concise and calm.

A **nimated eyes** Look directly into the camera. Flirt with it!

V **oice energy** Projection matters on TV. It's not about loudness but energy. Be yourself in a really upbeat good mood and send the energy to the back wall. You don't need masses of volume on a mic but you always need to project the thought to the viewer.

I **nspired** Passion comes across well on camera. Choose subjects that inspire you and talk about them passionately.

T **all** Sit up tall and slightly forward. Think of a long, straight spine.

A **rms** TV cameras can't cope with arm movements that are too big. The area between the chin and breastbone, no wider than the shoulders, is best as it allows you to gesture without being distracting as your hands move off camera.

S **mile** The camera loves a natural smile, especially those that start in the mind and move to the eyes. Think of an old friend and smile at them. The broadcaster's trick for charismatic likeability is to imagine you have a lovely secret. If you want to borrow from A-list actors you can add to this 'I'm beautiful, someone loves me, I have a secret'. This is a Royal Academy of Dramatic Art tip. It's cheesy but oh so effective for on-air sparkle.

Be Who You Are

The real trick to TV is to be yourself with oomph – you on a really good day. In the box opposite Jon Snow explains how it works.

Video Conferences

When it comes to Skype these rules can all be toned down. But when it's a formal video conference and you need to make a great impression, you're on camera in a context that matters. So step up and apply the skills in this section. It's all about being your best self – upright, eyes bright, concise and projected. If you're using notes, make sure that you don't look down at them too much. And remember to talk to a friend. Keep your voice and facial expression friendly and warm.

Project Your Energy

*People often say to me that they like that the person
that I am off air is the same as the person I am on air.
The only difference between the person on air and off air is
projection. The camera doesn't require a change of character.
You just have to work that little bit harder in terms of the
projection of your voice. Having been a choirboy as a child
and having had to sing to the back of a very long
nave has helped me a lot!*

*The key thing on air is to remember to relax because
you're usually full of adrenalin. It can help to imagine you
are talking to one person rather than 1.2 million people – if
you were thinking that you wouldn't do it! I imagine that
the viewer and I are going on a shared journey of discovery;
come along with me, come and see what we've just been looking
at. Sometimes it can be emotionally very powerful indeed.
I do think you have to allow yourself to get caught up in the
emotion, but at the same time it's no good milking it
or artificialising it – it either happens or it doesn't.*

JON SNOW, JOURNALIST AND PRESENTER

Conclusion – Falling Upwards

Be humble for you are made of dung
Be noble for you are made of stars
SERBIAN PROVERB

Gravitas is about falling upwards. The oppositional forces so key to gravity have much to teach us about gravitas. Your gravitas is all about tuning into the down-ness that gives you stability and trust in yourself, and the up-ness that allows you to have ease, lightness and openness to others. Then you can rise in your career even as you keep your feet firmly planted on the ground. It's a winning combination in life.

You already have gravitas. I hope this book has helped you understand that your job is to reveal your inner knowledge, power and passion above all. You have in your hands a useful reference to come back to time and time again when you need a reminder.

Gravitas can only improve with age. Its richness and texture comes from lived wisdom. There can be no rushing this, you just have to give in to experience. As the Greek poet laureate C. P. Cavafy writes in his poem 'Ithaka' (referencing Homer's *Odyssey*) 'better if it lasts for years, so you're wise by the time you reach the island'.

In the end, it all comes back to the gravitas equation:

Knowledge + purpose + passion (– anxiety) = Gravitas

Knowledge, purpose and passion can all continue to grow for as long as you are around on the planet. As the saying goes, growing older is compulsory, but growing up is a choice. The wisdom inherent in growing up is where gravitas flourishes, even as the forces of gravity pull you back down to earth. When it comes to gravitas, life really does begin at 40. In the second half of life we really get to step into gravitas. It's almost as if the first part of our lives is about building an outer container for gravitas in our early careers and then we grow into it with wisdom and humility in the second part.

The Practice of Gravitas

We do not think ourselves into new ways of living,
we live ourselves into new ways of thinking.
RICHARD ROHR, WRITER

There's always a gravitas in stillness. Finding it is simple. To come back to gravitas at any moment, come back to gravity. Go back to the FOFBOC – feet on floor, bottom on chair (see Principle 1 on page 30) and in the words of Franz Kafka,

> You do not need to leave your room. Remain sitting at your table and listen. Do not even listen, simply wait, be quiet, still and solitary. The world will freely offer itself to you to be unmasked, it has no choice, it will roll in ecstasy at your feet.[1]

Gravitas is there, available to you, as easily as gravity, if you are mindful, present, grounded. All you have to do is trust it. Allow it.

Do something little every day and you will look back after a few weeks, months and years and see how far you've come. That is what the seven principles combined with the practical rules for the big five are designed to help you do. To move gently yet powerfully forward in your life.

Mastery in any skill takes practice. My tip is to come back to these seven principles regularly. Make it fun. Little and often is key. Perhaps revise one at a time and use the Try This exercises as a way to practise. The ultimate aim? I want you to get the skills so deeply in the muscle that you can forget about them – that they become you.

When one of the big five challenges presents itself come back to the book – hopefully by now it is well thumbed – and remember that …

Intention + Attention = Result

If you do this and get these skills in the muscle you will be firmly en route to gravitas. And you will find that gravitas makes a massive difference to the trajectory of your life. People listen to what you say. You become a thought leader.

How You Have Value

You are not here merely to make a living. You are here to enrich the world … you impoverish yourself if you forget this errand.
WOODROW WILSON, PRESIDENT OF USA

The fire of gravitas is in its purpose. I believe that everyone has value that can help others and that gravitas is best expressed in that value.

Above all, celebrate what you already have, before refining your skills. When the poet, author and campaigner Dr Maya Angelou was a young woman, her mother helped celebrate who she was. One day, as they walked back together to the streetcar, Angelou's mother said, 'Wait a minute baby, you know, I think you're the greatest woman

I've ever met, along with Eleanor Roosevelt and my mother. You're in that category.'

What Dr Angelou's mother did, quite brilliantly, was to help her daughter believe that she had something to offer. Maya Angelou's knowledge, purpose and passion fired up with that self-belief. As Angelou explains, that young girl got into the streetcar with a new sense of possibility. 'I can remember how the sun fell on the slants of the wooden seats. Suppose she's right … she's says she's too mean to lie. Suppose I am going to be somebody? … She released me to say I may have something in me that would be of value … maybe not just to me … that's love.'[2]

Sometimes you don't have anyone to celebrate you. In those moments come back to yourself. Trust your true north. Do what you are here to do. Release your knowledge, your purpose, your passion. And remember – always, always, always carry yourself with authority.

We never know how high we are / Till we are called to rise; /
And then, if we are true to plan, / Our statures touch the skies—
EMILY DICKINSON, POET

Onwards and upwards!

Work with Caroline

I would make emotional intelligence, along with public speaking, a much bigger part of education. To be aware of one's subtle feelings, responses and desires, and to be able to articulate them well, are truly great gifts.

GRAYSON PERRY, *PROSPECT* MAGAZINE

If you'd like additional resources on video to help you integrate your skills I highly recommend that you go online to www.gravitasmethod.com. Sometimes it helps to hear and see the skills on video and audio and that's exactly why I've created them for you. You'll find free videos on a number of the areas I've covered in the book and also other training resources that will help you build on these skills and get them into the muscle.

There's also an online training programme for individuals and companies in the pipeline. Do sign up at www.gravitas method.com or follow @carolinegoyder on Twitter and we'll keep you posted.

If you'd like to let me know how you're getting on, if you have questions about how to develop the skills or if you'd like to arrange training or bring me in as a speaker for your organisation or event, please do email info@gravitasmethod.com.

I look forward to hearing about your successes as you find more and more of your innate gravitas.

Endnotes

Roots and Wings: What Exactly is Gravitas and How Can it Help You Succeed?

1. Dweck, CS, *Mindset: How You Can Fulfil Your Potential*, Constable & Robinson Limited (2012)
2. Feintzberg, R, 'Women, Men and the Gravitas Question', 'At Work' blog, *Wall Street Journal*, (Aug 2013)
3. Hewlett, SA, 'Center for Talent Innovation Executive Presence Study' (2012)
4. Dweck, CS, *Mindset: How You Can Fulfil Your Potential*, Constable & Robinson Limited (2012); Dweck, CS, *Self-theories: Their Role in Motivation, Personality and Development*, (Philadelphia), Psychology Press (1999)
5. Dweck, CS, Chiu, C; Hong Y, 'Implicit Theories and Their Role in Judgements and Reactions: A World from Two Perspectives'. *Psychological Enquiry* 6 (1995) 267–285

The Gravitas Equation: How Gravitas Works and How to Find Yours

1. Aristotle, *The Art of Rhetoric*, Penguin Classics (1991)

Field Guide to Gravitas: How to Spot Gravitas in Those Around You – the First Step to Finding it in Yourself

1. Noonan, P, *On Speaking Well: How to Give a Speech with Style, Substance, and Clarity* (New York), ReganBooks/Harper Perennial (1999)

Part One: The Seven Principles of Gravitas

Principle 1: Know Yourself – How to Build Your Inner Strength and Stability

1. Ekman, P, *Emotions Revealed: Recognizing Faces and Feelings to Improve Communication and Emotional Life*, Times Books (2003)

2. http://mindfulnessinschools.org/wp-content/uploads/2013/02/MiSP-Research-Summary-2012.pdf

3. Cicero (Miller, Walter trans.), *De Officiis,* The Loeb Classical Library, William Heinemann Ltd. (London); Harvard University Press (Cambridge, MA) (1975) Vol. XXI

4. www.kcbaker.com

5. Campbell, J, *Joseph Campbell and the Power of Myth with Bill Moyers*, edited by Betty Sue Flowers, Doubleday and Co, (1988), p120

6. Extract from Michael Palin's BBC programme on David Attenborough *Life on Air* (2002)

7. Descartes, R, *Discourse on the Method of Rightly Conducting One's Reason and of Seeking Truth in the Sciences* (1637)

8. Hawhee, D, *Bodily Arts: Rhetoric and Athletics in Ancient Greece*, University of Texas Press (Austin) (2004)

9. www.marieforleo.com, extract from 'How to overcome fear and shyness' (2013)

10. www.committedimpulse.com

11. Roosevelt, E, *You Learn by Living; Twelve Keys to a more Fulfilling Life*, Harper Perennial (1960)

Principle 2: Teach People How to Treat You – How to Balance Status and Connection So Others Respect You and Like You

1. See the work of Michael Grinder (www.michaelgrinder.com) for his ideas on status and connection, and his metaphor of 'Cat and Dog' to explain the difference

2. Weber, M, (trans. AR, Anderson and T Parsons), *Theory of Social and Economic Organization*. Chapter: 'The Nature of Charismatic Authority and its Routinization' (1947)

3. Tannen, D, *You Just Don't Understand: Men and Women in Conversation,* Ballantine (1990)

4. Carney, Dana R; Cuddy, Amy JC; Yap, AJ, 'Power Posing – Brief Nonverbal Displays Affect Neuroendocrine Levels and Risk Tolerance', *Journal of the Association for Psychological Science* 21 (10), (Oct 2010) 1363–1368

5. Carter, C; Macdonald, A; Ursu, S; Stenger, A; Ho Sohn, M; Anderson, J, 'How the brain gets ready to perform', presented at the 30th Annual Meeting of the Society of Neuroscience (New Orleans) (Nov 2000)

Principle 3: Find Your Voice: How to Communicate with Originality and Clarity

1. Pope, A, *An Essay on Criticism* (1711)
2. Roosevelt, E, *You Learn by Living; Twelve Keys to a more Fulfilling Life*, Harper Perennial (1960)
3. Noonan, P, *On Speaking Well*, William Morrow (1999)
4. Maslow, AH, *The Further Reaches of Human Nature*, Penguin Compass, New York, (1971) p180
5. www.kcbaker.com
6. Dobelli, R, *The Art of Thinking Clearly* (2013)
7. Ericsson, KA; Krampe, R; Tesch Romer, C, 'The Role of Deliberate Practice in the Acquisition of Expert Performance'. *Psychological Review* (1993), Vol 100. No 3, pp363–406
8. Collins, P, *The Art of Speeches and Presentations*, Wiley (2012)
9. Noonan, P, *On Speaking Well*, William Morrow (1999)
10. Fraisse, P, 'Rhythm and Tempo', in Deutsch, D (ed.), *The Psychology of Music* Academic Press (London) (1982)
11. Cole, H, *The New Republic* (1976) responding to a reading by Robert Lowell recorded live at 92Y on December 8, 1976. Lowell ended the night with 'Epilogue,' saying that a poem has to be more than memory, 'and yet memory, we're told, is the mother of the muses. Memory is genius – but you have to do something with it.'
12. www.kcbaker.com
13. Orwell, G, *Politics and The English Language* (1946)

Principle 4: Speak So Others Listen – How to Speak with Impact, Authority and Power

1. Churchill, Winston S, 'The Scaffolding of Rhetoric', (www.winstonchurchill.org) (1897)
2. 'New research casts doubt on value of student evaluations of professors', *The Chronicle of Higher Education* (1998)
3. Benki, JR; Broome, J; Conrad, F; Groves, R; Kreuter, F, 'Effects of Speech Rate, Pitch, and Pausing on Survey Participation Decisions', presented at the AAPOR Meeting, (University of Phoenix) (University of Michigan) (May 2011)

Principle 5: Win Hearts and Minds – How to Inspire, Engage and Influence Your Audience

1. Cicero, *On the Ideal Orator*, Book 2, 310 LOEB
2. Jack, AI; Dawson, AJ; Begany, KL; Leckie, RL; Barry, KP; Ciccia, AH; Snyder, AZ, 'MRI reveals reciprocal inhibition between social and physical cognitive domains', Department of Cognitive Science, Case Western Reserve University, Cleveland; Department of Psychological Sciences, Case Western Reserve University, Cleveland (2012)
3. Dilts, RB; DeLozier, JA, *Encyclopedia of Systemic Neuro-Linguistic Programming and NLP New Coding*, NLP University Press (2000)
4. Freytag, G, *Die Technik Des Dramas (Technique of the Drama: An Exposition of Dramatic Composition and Art)*, 1863
5. Zak, PJ, *The Moral Molecule, The Source of Love and Prosperity*, Dutton (2012); Kosfield, M; Heinrichs, M; Zak, PJ; Fischbacker, U; Fehr, E, 'Oxytocin increases Trust in Humans', *Nature* 435 (7042) (2005) 673–676
6. www.brenebrown.com

Principle 6: Keep an Open Mind and a Level Head – How to be Understanding and Influential Around Tricky People

1. Adapted from a story in Zander B, *The Art of Possibility*, Harvard Business Press (2002)
2. Satir, V, *Peoplemaking*, Souvenir Press Ltd (1972/1990)
3. Silver, N; Gottman, J, *Why Marriages Succeed or Fail: What You Can Learn From the Breakthrough Research to Make your Marriage Last*, Simon & Schuster (New York) (1994)
4. Fisher, R; Ury, W, *Getting To Yes*, Random House Business Books (New York) (1981)
5. Kegan, R; Laskow Lahey, L, *Immunity to Change: How to Overcome it and Unlock Potential in Yourself and Your Organization*, Harvard Business Press (Boston) (2009)
6. Zak, PJ, *The Moral Molecule*, Bantam Press (2012)
7. Fehmi, L; Robbins, J, *The Open-Focus Brain*, Trumpeter (2008)

Principle 7: Get Results – The Mirror, Signal, Manoeuvre of Success

1. Lamott, A, *Bird by Bird: Some Instructions on Writing and Life*, Anchor (1995)

2. Zimbardo, P; Boyd, J, *The Time Paradox: The New Psychology of Time that Will Change Your Life,* Free Press (2009)
3. Gollwitzer, PM, 'Implementation Intentions – Strong Effects of Simple Plans', *American Psychologist* 54 (7) (1999) 493–503
4. Freedman, L, 'Underdogs Take Heart – There is a Key to Victory', *The Sunday Times, Review* (Apr 2013)
5. Hawhee, D, *Bodily Arts, Rhetoric and Athletics in Ancient Greece,* University of Texas Press (2004)
6. Childre, D, Institute of HeartMath, www.heartmath.org, (1998)

Part Two: Gravitas in Action

Presentations and Talks

1. Duarte, N, *Resonate: Present Visual Stories That Transform Audiences,* Wiley (2010)
2. Anderson, C, 'How to Give a Killer Presentation', *Harvard Business Review* (June 2013)
3. Dilts, R, 'Strategies of Genius', Vol 1, *Meta Pubns,* (1995)

Meetings

1. Roosevelt, E, *You Learn by Living; Twelve Keys to a more Fulfilling Life,* Harper Perennial (1960)
2. Esler, G, *Lessons From the Top,* Profile Books (2012)

Telephone Calls and Teleconferences

1. Drahota, A; Costall, A; Reddy, V, 'The Vocal Communication of Different Kinds of Smile', *Speech Communication* (2007)
2. Ohala, JJ, 'The Acoustic Origin of the Smile', Phonology Laboratory, Department of Linguistics, University of California (1984)

Interviews and Pitches

1. Disney, W, *Growing Pains* (1941)

Conclusion

1. Kafka, F, *Aphorisms* (1918)
2. Dr Maya Angelou, 'Love Liberates', YouTube

Selected Further Reading and Videos

Atkinson, M, *Lend Me Your Ears*, Vermilion (2004)
A classic, must-read on the structure of good public speaking and presentation.

Collins, P, *The Art of Speeches and Presentations*, Wiley (2012)
A clear guide to making good presentations, by an experienced speech-writer, that draws on the rhetorical tradition.

Duarte, N, *Resonate: Present Visual Stories That Transform Audiences*, Wiley (2010)
An inspiring guide to structuring powerful presentations, using the principles of the dramatic arc.

Dweck, Carol, S, *Mindset: How You Can Fulfil Your Potential*, Robinson (2006)
A very readable guide from a world renowned Stanford Psychologist on how our mindset is key to success – and how to change it.

Forsyth, M, *The Elements of Eloquence: How to Turn The Perfect English Phrase*, (2013)
A lovely primer into crafting sentences with style – drawing on the rhetorical tradition.

Humes, JC, *Speak Like Churchill, Stand Like Lincoln*, Three Rivers Press (2002)
A great guide to public speaking from the speech-writer to five US Presidents.

Leith, S, *You Talkin' To Me? Rhetoric From Aristotle to Obama*, Profile Books (2012).
A thorough overview of the persuasive side of the rhetorical tradition, as opposed to delivery.

Satir, V, *Peoplemaking, Science and Behavior Books* (1972)
A wonderful book on the art of good relationships – and on being a leveller in life.

Videos

Josh Pais's great resources on www.committedimpulse.com are fantastic for presence and gravitas.

KC Baker's great website www.kcbaker.com is full of good resources for gravitas, with a focus on women.

And of course my site www.gravitasmethod.com has lots to support the book.

Acknowledgements

Books are team efforts. The team involved in the creation of this one have been stellar and taught me an immense amount. My heartfelt thanks go to all of you.

This book had a long genesis. The original idea came from David Young and Debbie Copping at BT who commissioned training on gravitas and started the whole thought process. It wouldn't have happened without you!

At Arvon, Hephzibah Anderson and Will Hodgkinson were inspiring and focusing tutors. Thank you for starting me on my way. To Claire Berliner and Oliver Meek for hosting and curating the bookworm's heaven that is Totleigh Barton.

Then the brilliant Sam Jackson came into the picture, via a baby-related serendipity. Sam's vision and sculpting of the book has been a revelation and I have learnt a huge amount from her. As a copy-editor Clare Hubbard's eye for detail has been thoughtful and transformative.

Jenny Nabben was my writing therapist as we circled Clapham Common after long writing days. Thank you for sage advice and fantastic friendship!

Jonny Geller and Kirsten Foster at Curtis Brown have been an incredible source of wise counsel and vision, full of much-needed practical solutions to the inevitable, occasionally mountainous, challenges of getting a book published. And Alice Dill has been of great support when it comes to the intricacies of contracts.

Claire Scott and Sue Amaradivakara have been PR wizards. I have massively appreciated your advice and insight in getting the word out.

Amy Gadney is the best first reader a girl could dream of and a wonderful friend. Thank you!

I want to say a massive thank you to all those who contributed to the research for the book, both those who kindly agreed to be named and who feature throughout the book, and also those who I spoke to who for professional reasons felt it was better to remain anonymous. You all inspired and focused the research. For that I am hugely grateful.

And most importantly of all I want to say thank you to my nearest and dearest, my fantastic family and my dear, dear friends. You know who you are. You are rocks. And you rock. I couldn't have finished this without your love and support and the occasional glass of wine. Thank you.

Index